THE FIRE
OF GOD

DISCOVERING ITS MANY
LIFE-CHANGING PURPOSES

JOY DAWSON

Destiny Image strives for excellence in all its publications. Although every effort has been made to provide full documentation of all sources used in this text, some references and source material were not available for review and attribution. If you are familiar with a reference in this text for which the source material is not available in the "Endnotes," please feel free to forward such information to Destiny Image.

Destiny Image₍ᵣ₎ Publishers, Inc.
P.O. Box 310
Shippensburg, PA 17257-0310

"Speaking to the Purposes of God for This Generation and for the Generations to Come"

ISBN 10: 0-7684-2622-7;

ISBN 13: 978-07684-2622-9

For Worldwide Distribution
Printed in the U.S.A.

This book and all other Destiny Image, Revival Press, MercyPlace,Fresh Bread, Destiny Image Fiction, and Treasure House books are availableat Christian bookstores and distributors worldwide.

Softcover 1 2 3 4 5 6 7 8 9 10 / 10 09 08

For a U.S. bookstore nearest you, call **1-800-722-6774.**
For more information on foreign distributors, call: **717-532-3040.**
Or reach us on the Internet: **www.destinyimage.com**

ACKNOWLEDGMENTS

I have written six books, but never have I had less understanding about what I was going to write than I have with this one, and that includes before I started and all the way through. All I had were two messages I had given on "The Fire of God," when the Holy Spirit directed me to write a book on that subject, with the understanding that there were also other aspects that would have to be included.

Never have I been on such a remarkable writing journey of faith. I would sit at my desk with a pen and blank sheets of paper and my Bible. Consistently, as I would bow my head and heart before God and acknowledge that I had no clue what to write, and then thank Him that He did, and believe that He would direct me, the flow of words would come into my mind, and I would write— by the hour. There was also a well of truth inside me from which the Holy Spirit could draw and bring to my remembrance, from decades of pursuing Him who is the Truth.

As I would turn to a familiar verse of Scripture to validate a point, suddenly the Holy Spirit would open up my understanding to truths surrounding it that I had never seen. This became standard procedure, for which I would marvel and worship God.

It has been a delight to work with the wonderfully cooperative Destiny Image staff for whom I am deeply grateful.

I am also acutely aware that this was occurring as a result of my dear intercessor friends with whom I had shared my great need for prayer support. To them I give my sincerest thanks, heartfelt gratitude, and love. God will undoubtedly reward them.

My deepest appreciation also goes to my precious life partner and best friend, Jim, who has taken my handwritten scripts and put them into the computer. His listening ear, helpful comments, strong encouragement, and many prayers have been invaluable.

I know dear Lord
that You love me;
You've proved it so
at Calvary
My love for You
is proved, You've said,
But my obedience
to Your Word.

I'll trust You Lord
when I can't see
the way ahead
that's best for me.
I know You'll guide
me all the way.
Just tell me Lord
and I'll obey.

I put my life
in Your dear hands.
With joy I'll follow
Your commands.
I know it's only
by Your grace,
I will endure
and run the race.

*And when I look
into Your eyes
that burn with love
and holy fire,
my deep desire
is that You'll see
You truly had
Your way with me.*

TABLE OF CONTENTS

The Fire of God in Testing

Want to know God?

He's not impressed or intimidated by heat. He made it. He can control it or be immune from it. He's fireproof. One day He suddenly showed up when three of His friends were thrown into a blazing inferno. The heat was so fierce that the guys who were assigned the job of disposing of the three men were burned to a crisp in the process. God not only totally, miraculously insulated His friends from the effect of the flames, but He actually walked around with them in the middle of the furnace. I call Him "Mr. Cool." The four of them were so oblivious to the deathly heat, and were as relaxed as poached eggs, that it blew the mind of the tyrant head of state who had ordered their incineration—to the point that he made it mandatory for everyone in his kingdom to recognize and worship only this God. (You can check out this story in Daniel 3:19-29.) God is definitely something else (or Someone else)—other worldly. He excites me.

Want to know more?

A young man named G.W. Hardcastle (known by all his family and friends as "G"), having clearly heard the call of God to enter Bible college to train to become a pastor, initially responded positively but then decided to do his own thing. Like Jonah, G disobeyed the call. And like Jonah, he ended up in a horrendous situation.

While working for an electrical company, he was assigned the job of assisting a foreman who was running in new cables from a substation to a service pole over a block away. G's job was to go to the substation, climb a ladder, and find the new cable. Using a battery tester, he was supposed to put just enough electricity in the new cable to cause a light to shine on each phase so his boss could tag them.

When the foreman gave the signal to begin, G mistakenly took hold of the wrong cable. Instantly, 4,160 volts held him in a searing, electrifying ball of flame. The rate of amperage was tremendously high and the blast was so terrific that it knocked him backward and he found himself hanging by his right leg, head down. His whole body felt like a piece of wax paper in a furnace, in excruciating pain.

The doctors' report to his parents was that if G lived, which was unlikely, he would probably have no use of his arms or legs, and his ears, nose, and lips would be gone for the rest of his life—a drawn, distorted mass of flesh. G's father was a pastor who asked and believed God, not only for the miracle of life for his son, but for the miracle of complete healing—total restoration of every damaged area of his body.

On the third day after the accident, G's temperature rose past the critically dangerous level and the doctors again predicted death. G was delirious with pain and had to be held down by several people. Then he felt death coming on. Still, the father prayed and believed God. An amazing miracle took place as he laid his hand on his son's head in prayer. G instantly fell asleep! Only after he woke did the doctors state that it seemed as though the boy had survived the death crisis.

In the long, dark, painful months that followed, while G lay in the hospital covered in bandages, he totally surrendered his life and future to God and said he would obey Him, no matter what.

When the long-awaited day came for the bandages to be removed, the doctor exclaimed, "My God, son, this is a miracle," and kept repeating it. The doctors had previously concluded that not only would G be devoid of nose, lips, ears, and facial features, but they expected massive infections. The irrefutable fact was that not only were all his features and arms and legs in perfect condition, but his skin was like a newborn baby's—perfect. Although over 75 percent of G's body had been subjected to mostly third-degree burns, the doctors had no explanation for the lack of scars.

The young man trained and in time became a wonderful pastor. Throughout his life he said that one small scar remained on his right hand as a constant reminder of God's call upon his life, His miraculous power to heal, and His unending mercy.

G Hardcastle learned that being in the searing furnace of pain was what God allowed to get his attention, to show him that he was walking away from his destiny. But the miraculous grace of God's pursuing love and healing power was far greater than the fiery trial and ultimately was the means of his fulfilling his God-ordained destiny.

Even more amazing to me is the next story. This same awesome God allowed one of His young friends to have one side of his face blown off in the bloody ravages of the Vietnam War. And the horrific scars were not, and still are not, erased. But the young soldier's faith and proven friendship with this same God, my God, have never been fazed. The fact that this war veteran looks like a monster, the sort that Hollywood would create to scare you spitless, hasn't deterred him one iota from fulfilling his God-ordained destiny. Just the reverse. Dave Roever travels extensively and is frequently seen on television programs. He has a passion, and it shines through the scars. It's a fervent love for this same God, and a burning desire for people—especially young people—to believe in Him and know Him. This warrior champions for God vocally, and people listen!

We're forced to make rational conclusions. This same God, the God and Father of our Lord Jesus Christ, the God of the Bible is so absolutely compelling and amazingly wonderful that whether we're miraculously delivered in the midst of the fire, or miraculously healed from the effects of the fire, or permanently scarred by the effects of the fire, His unfathomable love never leaves us, and His presence and enabling power to endure and overcome is available to us, big time, all the time!

What a God! I've been turned on to Him for over seven decades. I asked Him to take over my life and do His thing in me and through me when I was a child of five. He's still doing both. And He's definitely Mr. Cool, no matter how sizzling hot the temperature of the circumstances.

None of us who want to be close to God can escape the heat—first, because of who God is. *"Our God is a consuming fire"* (Hebrews 12:29). And Mark 9:49 says, *"For everyone will be seasoned with fire...."* When we come to grips with these two statements of truth and accept their reality, we will be far less perplexed when the temperature of life's circumstances escalates—sometimes alarmingly.

Know God. Expect heat. It's that simple.

Contained fires have a compelling and unique fascination. They give warmth and comfort and distinctive beauty. Because our God is a consuming fire He has all those attractions and functions. It couldn't be otherwise. There's a magnetic attraction to a contained fire. We instinctively want to get close. The same thing happens when we want to get serious about knowing God intimately.

The truths in this book about the many aspects of the fire of God are intended to ignite our passion for an intense love relationship with the most awesome, intriguing, fascinating, and at times, mysterious Being in the universe—Lover God—and to really experience Him as such.

But, for this all-fulfilling relationship to develop, it's imperative that we understand and embrace every aspect of this "*consuming fire*" God. The closer we get to Him in friendship, and *stay* near Him, the more clearly we understand how important, in fact *crucial*, is every aspect of the fire of God in our lives experientially. To dodge any aspect by not studying it from the Bible, or to be non-cooperative with God as He takes us into any aspect of it, or to be casual about the subject as a whole, will inevitably mean missing the fulfillment of our God-ordained destinies.

We know that God is love, God is light, God is life, and we rightly embrace those realities. He is no less a consuming fire, so we need to embrace that reality with equal certainty and security. That is, of course, if we're deadly serious about getting as close to Him as He will allow.

I believe, as God's children, we're all either in a fiery trial (with varying degrees of heat), heading for one and don't know it, or have been in one and need more understanding of how to get through the next one more successfully. I believe the degree of the heat of God's fire in each believer's life is proportionate to the extent of God's plan to use each one for the extension of His Kingdom and to bring glory to the name of the Lord Jesus Christ. This is vividly illustrated in the lives of Job, Abraham, Joseph, David, Daniel, Mordecai, Esther, Jeremiah, Mary, Paul, and the apostle John. In each case the intense heat came when they were living righteous lives before God and men. This means we must never presume on God's purposes for those in the fire. We must never judge.

Our Initial Reaction to the Fire

Our initial reaction to the fire of God in testing is crucial. It is of paramount importance to understand the character of God in relation to this aspect of His fire. First, we must understand that none of our trials have taken Him by surprise. He knows exactly what's going on and hasn't forgotten our address. In fact, in Jeremiah 12:3, God tells us that He is actively involved in the testing process of His children: *"But You, O Lord, know me; You have seen me, and You have tested my heart toward You."*

Second, we must realize that as God allows the difficult circumstances to continue in order to test our reactions to them, He is absolutely just, righteous, and kind.

"For the righteous God tests the hearts and minds (Psalm 7:9).
*The Lord is just in **all** His ways, and kind in **all** His doings"* (Psalm 145:17 RSV).

The more we study the justice of God from His Word, the more readily we'll be able to receive by faith His grace to cope in the heat of the fiery trial, with peace of mind. It will keep us from succumbing to the temptation of resenting God that He ever allowed us to be in the fire of testing in the first place—especially if the trial is lengthy, and sometimes it is.

From deep personal experience, I periodically remind myself of the insanity of resenting total justice and unfathomable love! Worship and trust are the only sane responses. And to the degree that I embrace the heat and realize that He is controlling the temperature, I can be assured that His additional rewards and blessings are an inevitable expression of His justice when the tests are passed. In short, we'll always get a fair deal when we're submitted to a righteous, just God who says, "*For I know the thoughts that I think toward you, says the Lord, thoughts of peace and not of evil, to give you a future and a hope*" (Jeremiah 29:11).

Just before Moses died, he gave the children of Israel an important, lengthy song about God's character and ways, which they were to heed and command their children to obey so that God could bless them. It is very significant that the first attributes to which Moses drew their attention were God's greatness and justice. I don't know a more convincing verse on the justice of God than Deuteronomy 32:4: "*He is the Rock, His work is perfect; for all His ways are justice, a God of truth and without injustice; righteous and upright is He.*"

Having established that we're in the hands of a God who is totally trustworthy in character, the following four prayers get our priorities in order. They have proved to be immensely helpful to me.

First, determine in your heart and express it to God that no matter what it costs and how long you're in the fiery trial, you want Him to receive the maximum glory that can come to His wonderful name. This prayer determines in a hurry whether we're really living for God's glory or for our own agenda and comfort. I invite you to pray Paul's prayer in Philippians 1:20 (RSV): "*As it is my eager expectation and hope that I shall not be at all ashamed, but that with full courage now as always Christ will be honored in my body, whether by life or death."*

Second, ask God to use the trial to bring you into a more intimate relationship with Himself and a more passionate love for the Lord Jesus.

Third, ask Him to reveal to you what He wants to teach you related to any causes and purposes for the fire.

Fourth, seek God for direction as to any course of action you are to take, believing Psalm 32:8 (RSV), *"I will instruct you and teach you the way you should go; I will counsel you with My eye upon you."*

These responses line us up immediately with God's highest purposes, and when answered, will ultimately bring the greatest blessings to our lives.

When answers to the above prayers are delayed we need to be aware that at times God may hide Himself from us, in order to test our faith.

Truly, You are a God who hides Himself, O God of Israel, the Savior (Isaiah 45:15 RSV).

And I will wait on the Lord, who hides His face from the house of Jacob; and I will hope in Him (Isaiah 8:17).

No other book in the Bible gives us more understanding of the ways of God in testing than the Book of Job. Apart from the horrendous loss of his children, his cattle, his servants, a house, his health, and his wife's support, he had the toughest of all tests: the perplexity test. Remember, Job had no Bible, no supportive spiritual leaders, friends, or family, and no clue why God had allowed the chaos and pain or why He was silent. That's the total pits in my reckoning!

But, no other book shouts more loudly and clearly that although satan was permitted by God to put "the most righteous man in all the earth" in this blazing bonfire of circumstances, God, not the devil, was ultimately in control of the heat. ***Because God is always in control***. Period. As He reminds us in Psalm 46:10: "*Be still, and know that I am God*."

And because God is unswervingly faithful, perfectly righteous, unfathomably loving, and absolutely just, God's purposes were finally to bless Job with such an overdose of His lavish, abundant goodness, that it made his life before the testing look like a pauper's life. *That's God!*

By far the greatest thing we can have to keep our faith strong in the fires of God's testing is the revelation of each of God's characteristics. There's only one way to obtain that understanding. It's by studying them, one by one, from God's Word. And there are no shortcuts or crash courses!

God will allow Christians, non-Christians, natural disasters, suffering, the difficulties that come from living in a fallen world, demons, principalities, and satan himself, if He chooses, to test our reactions. We either react according to the way God's Word tells us to, and then pass the test, or we react contrary to what the Bible says, and fail the test.

Sometimes the biggest tests come through those with whom we live. It was so with Job. "*Then his wife said to him, 'Do you still hold fast to your integrity? Curse God and die'*" (Job 2:9). Obviously, Job's wife gave this grim advice because of her grave failure to pass the tests of her many losses. Basically, it was symptomatic of the lack of revelation of God's character and ways.

The one who should have been the most understanding, strongly supportive, encouraging person to Job in the furnace of affliction, his wife, actually took sides with satan and his plan to try to prove to God that Job only worshiped God because of all the blessings that surrounded his life. A life partner, observing his or her mate going through a fiery trial, can either be the biggest help or the biggest hindrance.

When the heat is turned up, people who observe their close friends in those circumstances will react and advise according to their knowledge of God's character and ways from His Word. If their knowledge is limited, they should be loving and helpful in practical ways. It would also be wise to ask God to send spiritual counsel from those who do have that knowledge, and keep their own mouths closed.

Can you imagine being covered in painful boils from your dandruff to your toenails, while a bunch of your supposed friends sit staring in total silence at you for the first week? And then, one by one, they deliver weighty and lengthy discourses as to why they were sure that the reason for all your pain and loss was because of un-dealt-with sin in your life. It would have been enough to turn all Job's boils into carbuncles!

It's no wonder that when God finally came on the scene He humbled Job's audience by telling them that the only way they could be reinstated into fellowship with God again was by depending on Job's ministry of intercession on their behalf.

Okay, so much for how *not* to act toward others when they are in the fires of God's testing. In my book, *Intercession, Thrilling and Fulfilling* I share the right way, in Chapter 3.

Two things are proved when we pass God's tests in difficult circumstances. First, it proves to God that we can be trusted to receive greater privileges and responsibilities in relation to the extension of His Kingdom. For example, when a motor company is advertising its latest vehicle, often we see a TV commercial with that vehicle being put through the most severe tests, being driven over rugged terrain in the worst weather conditions, yet the vehicle comes through as if it were made of granite. God works on the same principle. No pain, no gain. No tests, no promotion. Just as the motor company brags on the performance of its product, so God can brag on us before all the great *"cloud of witnesses"* referred to in Hebrews 12:1.

Second, we prove that as we react according to the Word of God in every difficult situation, and receive by faith His amazing grace, He is faithful and will do His part to carry us through. *"When you walk through the fire, you shall not be burned"* (Isaiah 43:2).

If we fail the tests, in His great love and spiritual ambition for us, God will set up or allow another lot of difficult circumstances in the hope that we will cooperate with Him and His ways—so that He can bless us more. *"But He knows the way that I take; when He has tried me, I shall come forth as gold"* (Job 23:10 RSV). And James 1:12 (RSV) says, *"Blessed is the man who endures trial, for when he has stood the test he will receive the crown of life which God has promised to those who love Him."*

The Way God Tests Our Motives

God is far more interested in our motives than our actions. So much so that He tells us that at the Judgment Seat, He will judge us according to *why* we did what we did. That's worth pondering.

What is our immediate reaction when someone else who has been equipped by God with similar ministry giftings or talents is put alongside of us in God's service, but they have less experience than we have and they are given more prominence and opportunities to minister?

What about when someone younger and less experienced is promoted to a leadership position above us? If we are truly living and ministering to others for God's glory alone, and have God's love in our hearts toward everyone around us, our immediate response will be to encourage them, intercede for them, and support them in every way possible. *"Do nothing from selfishness or conceit, but in humility count others better than yourselves"* (Philippians 2:3 RSV).

In fact, if we want to really enjoy the person and their ministry to the fullest extent, we can help to promote their ministry or talents. Now that's real freedom and, in fact, fun. Paul talks about it in Romans 12:9-10 (AMP) *"Let your love be sincere....Love one another with brotherly affection; giving precedent and showing honor to one another."*

However, I think one of the hardest tests that I have watched leaders battling through is when a senior leader has repeatedly failed in some area of leadership. God then requires that he promote a younger leader whom he may have trained for years to take his place. Harder still, God commands that the senior leader encourage the younger one.

The classic example of this scenario is Moses and Joshua. Listen to Moses' account of God's instructions to him in Deuteronomy 1:37-38: *"The Lord was also angry with me for your sakes, saying, 'Even you shall not go in there. Joshua the son of Nun, who stands before you, he shall go in there. **Encourage** him, for he shall cause Israel to inherit it."* Moses never earned his God-given commercial as *"the meekest man in all the earth"* (see Numbers 12:3 RSV) more, than when he passed his humility test by fully discharging God's mandate in this instance.

We read in Deuteronomy 3:26 that after Moses had pleaded with the Lord to let him go in and see the Promised Land, God said, *"Enough of that! Speak no more to Me of this matter."* In other words, *"I'm not going to change My mind on this issue."*

Then came the biggest test, in Deuteronomy 3:28, as God told Moses not only to *encourage* Joshua but to *strengthen* him. That means, become Joshua's greatest supporter and promoter, regardless of the fact that Moses, for many years, had taken the blazing heat of more leadership tests than Joshua could possibly remember or count. Moses' humility shone like a brilliant sunrise at dawn when he *"called Joshua and said to him in the sight of all Israel, 'Be strong and of good courage, for **you** must go with this people to the land which the Lord has sworn to their fathers to give them, and **you** shall cause them to inherit it"* (Deuteronomy 31:7).

The strengthening part continues as Moses goes on to say, *"'And the Lord, He is the One who goes before you. He will be with you, He will not leave you nor forsake you; do not fear nor be dismayed'"* (Deuteronomy 31:8). Well done, Moses. Leadership tests passed with honors. Instead of resenting God's choice of the leader in his place, and being jealous and critical of him, Moses became his primary supporter and enjoyed him. Pride and jealousy only distance us from others whom God promotes above us. Humility brings the benefits that accompany close fellowship with them. *"As for God, His way is perfect"* (Psalm 18:30). And that's always the way of the cross.

Another motive test is when God puts a younger person or a younger Christian or someone of another gender across our path who has experienced God or been used by God in ways that we may not. Will we be humble and thank God for the opportunity to learn from them? Will we encourage them? If, through pride and jealousy, we choose otherwise, then we're heading for real trouble for ourselves and them.

In First Kings 13, we read about a young man of God from Judah who was sent by God to Bethel to give a prophetic announcement in the Temple, which was followed by unusual displays of God's miracle-working power to confirm the message. An older prophet from the same town heard from his sons about the dynamic spiritual action that had taken place and made it his business to contact the younger man of God, inviting him to his home for a meal. The action looked spiritual but the motive was carnal.

The young man refused to accept the hospitality on the grounds that God had given him clear instructions not to eat or drink and to return home by a different route. The old prophet lied and replied that he too was a prophet and that God had spoken to him through an angel, that the younger man was to eat bread and drink water in his house. So he did.

What but horrible jealousy could have prompted that blatant lie and been the cause of tempting the young man to disobey God? You see, the older prophet's sons had already reported to their father that earlier in the day the king had offered hospitality to the young man and he had refused it because of not wanting to disobey God's instructions. The old prophet also knew that God's judgment always follows disobedience (see Deuteronomy 28:1-15; Leviticus 10:1-3; Leviticus 26). He obviously missed his integrity and humility tests.

The young man of God was also being tested by God through his encounter with the deceitful, older man. What should he have done? He should have thanked the old prophet for his offer of hospitality and then explained that it was totally contrary to God's mandate to him personally, therefore they both needed to seek God again, as God is not the author of confusion.

If the older prophet had not been willing to do this, it would have been an instant exposure of the pride of his heart. If they had both sought God, He would have gladly confirmed to the young man's spirit that he had heard from God correctly. Then, with the fear of the Lord upon him, which is the only thing that delivers us from the fear of man, the young prophet would have stated that he must obey what he firmly believed were God's personal instructions. Instead, his disobedience cost him his life (see 1 Kings 13:24). What a solemn warning.

If you, dear reader, are in a situation where someone senior in ministry experience or someone over you in authority insists on stating that he or she has guidance from God about your life that is contrary to what you sincerely believe (from having sought God's will yourself), I recommend the following:

- Humility is the greatest safeguard. Pride is the basis of all deception (see Obadiah 3).
- Always express gratitude for others' concerns for your life and walk with the Lord.
- Be completely open and willing to receive wise counsel from people with proven, godly character, who you know walk closely with the Lord Jesus and are strong in the knowledge of God's character and ways from His Word.
- Ask them if they would be willing to listen to both your convictions and the convictions of others who are speaking into your life.
- Pray that truth would prevail and believe God for the answer.
- Trust God that He will cause the Holy Spirit to disturb your spirit, if what you are sensing is not the mind of God. Equally trust Him to give you a deep-seated conviction and peace if what you are sensing is the will of God.
- Do spiritual warfare, commanding the forces of darkness to be bound and rendered impotent according to James 4:7, Revelation 12:11, and First John 3:8.
- Keep praising God and thanking Him that it is the Shepherd's responsibility to make the directions clear as to

which gate the sheep are to go through when the need arises (see John 10:3-4,27). We are His sheep.

• Keep asking for—and receiving by faith—the fear of the Lord, and then act in obedience to what you believe God has revealed to you. *"Who is the man that fears the Lord? Him shall He teach in the way He chooses"* (Psalm 25:12).

In my book, *Forever Ruined for the Ordinary*, I have written about the other side of the truth, where there are times in the Bible when people disobeyed God by not heeding the word of the Lord through others. This topic can be found in Section Six of that book.

One of the simplest ways that God can test whether our motives are purely for His glory is by seeing how we respond to His direction from the Word about an involvement in the ministry of intercession (which simply means praying as directed and energized by the Holy Spirit for others). Jesus teaches that it is mostly done in secret (see Matthew 6:6).

When we can pray frequently for others, including large projects or small, nations or world leaders, for short or long periods of time, and never feel the slightest need to tell anyone about it, we can know we have passed God's tests about the need for recognition.

In order to test our motives, God will direct us to be involved in many ministry-related situations where we will be active behind the scenes and receive little or no recognition and often little encouragement or appreciation. God is seeing how much He can trust us for future ministry assignments that are in His plan for our lives. In His wisdom He won't promote us until we've proved by the motive of our hearts that Ephesians 6:5-7 is a living reality: *"Be obedient to those who are your masters according to the flesh, with fear and trembling, in sincerity of heart, as to*

Christ; not with eyeservice, as men-pleasers, but as bondservants of Christ, doing the will of God from the heart, with goodwill doing service, as to the Lord, and not to men."

I well remember the years of joyous, fulfilling ministry—in food preparation and then setting up chairs and tables and fancy tablecloths—in readiness for the morning teas a few Christian women and myself would regularly put on. The purpose was to invite an interesting speaker who, with vital spiritual content, would address the gathering, which consisted of many Christian and non-Christian women. My husband and children would help me set up the tables and chairs the evening before the event, and I would invariably be one of the last to leave when all the cleanup was completed at the end of the event.

My only reason for mentioning this period of my life is to say that in those days I hadn't the slightest idea that one day I would be the invited speaker at many churches, training schools, and international conferences. Nothing could have been further from my mind. It needed to be that way so that God could see whether I would be totally fulfilled in consistently serving others at the unseen ground level...with delight. It also helped me to always deeply appreciate all the work and workers who are inevitably involved in every public ministry event where I have been the speaker.

We can never be trusted by God with prominence until we've learned to be content with obscurity. God is more impressed with motive than action. Any service for the Lord, no matter how menial, can become a joy-filled, meaningful assignment if we keep focused on the magnificent Master who has directed us to serve Him by serving others. After all, it was Jesus who introduced us to foot washing.

I remember a spiritual leader of real prominence telling me how, when he was a young man, he had hated it when the leaders over him would announce that the group would now have a foot washing ministry to each other. He said he used to wince inside. Looking back over the years, he shared how easily that same ministry has become to him, in fact, a joy. Humility had made the difference.

It's relatively unimportant what God tells us to do, whether it's commanding the dead to come to life or changing a baby's diapers, whether it's going to Saudi Arabia or cutting someone's toenails. The big deal is all about the One who gives the orders. When that conviction grips our hearts, we can truthfully, joyfully, say with certainty, *"Not unto us, O Lord, not unto us, but to Your name give glory, because of Your mercy, because of Your truth"* (Psalm 115:1). In other words, let's get impressed with the Who not the what. Our perspective of God's character makes the difference. And that applies to every situation, no matter what!

Difficult Circumstances

Some tests from God may come only once in a lifetime. Not this one. Jesus realistically stated that *"in the world you will have tribulation, but be of good cheer, I have overcome the world"* (John 16:33).

During times of persecution when Paul and Barnabas were strengthening and encouraging the early Christians, they said, *"We must through many tribulations enter the kingdom of God"* (Acts 14:22). King David said, from much experience, *"Many are the afflictions of the righteous, but the Lord delivers him out of them all"* (Psalm 34:19). The apostle Peter gave us a down-to-earth appraisal on life when he warned us, *"Do not be surprised at the fiery ordeal which comes upon you to prove you, as though something strange were happening to you. But rejoice in so far as you share Christ's sufferings, that you may also rejoice and be glad when His glory is revealed"* (1 Peter 4:12-13).

All of them basically say the same thing: It's often going to be a rough ride. But the Lord Jesus has already been over the road and not only knows where everything is positioned, from the potholes to the hidden mines, but will tell us how to navigate them. Better yet, He will come on the ride with us and actually take over if we'll let Him. You can't beat that for service!

We do ourselves a favor by getting a firm grip on the fact that fiery trials are an integral and inevitable part of our normal Christian experience. If we don't believe and understand that basic concept, we'll always be confused and frustrated, disappointed, and possibly bitter toward God when He sends or allows the fire of difficult circumstances.

Let's look back at those three verses of Scripture—because they not only have the realistic bad news but the realistic good news. And it's good news we need to major on, every time, all the time, and during overtime.

In John 16:33, Jesus tells us that the way to handle life's inevitable tribulations is to remember that Jesus, as Son of man, lived through more tribulations when He was on earth than we ever will. And by His death and resurrection He overcame the source of all evil and trouble. First John 3:8 says, *"For this purpose the Son of God was manifested, that He might destroy the works of the devil."*

"Okay," you say, "but how does that help me when I have to face life's daily difficulties?" Every way. When you completely surrender your life to the Lord Jesus and ask Him to daily fill you with His Spirit, and invite Him to think through your mind, look through your eyes, speak through your mouth, love through your heart, touch through your hands, walk through your feet, and believe that He will…He does.

So Jesus says, in effect, "In the midst of your tribulations, don't panic or get uptight or discouraged. I've been there. Experienced that. I'm Mr. Big. There's nothing that's got Me beat. I'm in control. I'm in you. So chill out and let Me live My life through you, by faith, moment by amazing supernatural moment."

Back to David's testimony. Basically it's that many bad things can happen to good people, but ultimately God rescues them in His way and time. That puts a smile of hope on our faces, a reminder of God's justice and faithfulness.

Now back to Peter's warning, because here's where we find out how we can cooperate with God while we're going through the tough stuff and the rewards that come when we do. The Holy Spirit inspired Peter to tell us to rejoice that we actually get the chance to share in a little of Christ's sufferings. You may say, "What in the world is the purpose of that?"

Well, we have to go and listen to Paul's intense heart cry to God as he expresses his desire to know God intimately, in Philippians 3:10: *"That I may know Him and the power of His resurrection, and the fellowship of His sufferings, being con-formed to His death."* Obviously Paul understood and many of Jesus' subsequent disciples have understood that when we ask for the fellowship of Christ's sufferings, we will inevitably have to suffer. That makes sense. It will happen either sooner or later if we're really serious about knowing God. If Jesus *"learned obedience by the things which He suffered"* (Hebrews 5:8), how much more do we need suffering in order to be made more like Him? Remember Peter said that the reward for rejoicing in shar-ing Christ's sufferings is that God will reveal His glory to us. That means as many of His characteristics as we're able to han-dle at given times. What an incredible privilege! Better yet, Paul tells us in Romans 8:18, *"that the sufferings of this present time are not worthy to be compared with the glory which shall be revealed in us."*

I can assure you from many years of deep personal experience that worshiping and praising God for who He is, as a way of life, in the furnace of affliction, keeps our minds at peace and enables us to receive by faith His amazing grace. It puts our focus on the ultimate positive, God Himself. And the negative can't survive in that environment.

The Rest of Faith

I now want to share with you, dear reader, another key principle to coping in difficult circumstances, which produces some pretty amazing results. It's how to have a practical workout with Psalm 37:5 (RSV): *"Commit your way to the Lord; trust in Him, and He will act."*

There are two things we have to do before we believe God will do His part. The first order is to commit the circumstances and everyone connected with them into God's hands. The Hebrew word for "commit" literally means "to throw." But we have difficulty in throwing our burdens completely until our hands are empty, until we understand how to fulfill the second order, which is to trust Him. This is where we concentrate on some of God's characteristics:

1. As a God of *all knowledge* He is aware of all the factors related to the problem.
2. As a God of *all wisdom* He knows how and when to solve it.
3. As a God of *absolute righteousness and justice* He will only do the right and just thing by everyone involved in the problem.
4. As a God of *all power* He is able to catch what we throw at Him.

5. As a God of *unfathomable love* He longs to catch and
   solve our problem.

Now we take in our hands some harmless object that represents our problem, like a cushion, and in the light of who God
is, we literally throw it away from us, and turn our backs on it.
Then we walk away as we thank and praise God in full faith that
He is acting according to His eternal, living Word.

This verse (Psalm 37:5), when applied to everyday circumstances, produces dramatic results. I've experienced it many times
myself and have seen it work for others. Remember, it's related to
testing times in difficult circumstances. Are we going to disregard
God's instructions and go on worrying and disappoint Him? Or
are we going to put His Word into action and watch Him work on
our behalf? The latter is infinitely more exciting, believe me.
Here's how it works.

I had finished giving the message at a Presbyterian women's
meeting in Auckland, New Zealand, and the meeting was closed
when an older lady approached me and asked for my counsel. Her
name was Mrs. Watkins, and she had a legitimate dilemma. She
had contracted to give board and lodging in her home for one
year to two Asian students of whom she was very fond. However,
she recently received a letter from her grandson in England, saying he really needed her and asked her to come and spend some
time with him. Mrs. Watkins sensed it was related to a spiritual
struggle he was having, and being a godly, caring grandmother,
she longed to go and help him.

What on earth was she to do? She felt bound to honor the
agreement with the fine young men for whom she was responsible. I listened in silence to the Holy Spirit for His wisdom to know
how to respond to this sincere Christian woman. His answer was
immediate. "Take her through the process in Psalm 37, verse 5." I

did, specifically asking that God would provide another Christian home for the students.

As I spoke out the different parts of God's character as they related to her problem, faith mounted. Then I took a harmless object in my hand, which represented the problem, and literally threw it away from us, thanking and praising God that because we were truly trusting Him, He was truly acting on our behalf.

A minute or two later, a young woman, Mrs. McKenzie, walked into an almost empty church looking puzzled. I asked if I could help her. She said, "I don't know. But I went to step inside my car to go home, and I had one foot on the ground and the other in the car, when I had a distinct impression come into my mind. 'Go back into the church,' so here I am." I said, "Then maybe you are part of what's going on here," and simply shared what had just taken place. I found that she was a Christian friend of Mrs. Watkins. "Oh, I think I have the answer," she said to her with a big smile. "My two little boys know your two Asian students and are very fond of them. I can easily take them into my home as boarders for as long as you need to be in England. I've been longing to have two Christian student boarders, just like yours."

WOW! At the precise moment we threw the problem at God and trusted Him, He acted.

The sequel to this story is that Mrs. Watkins was directed by God to go to England and was a great help to her grandson at a time of spiritual need. She was the means of his committing his life to Christ and getting him established in a strong church fellowship. Later, he became a medical missionary, and Mrs. Watkins was given a vital, fulfilling ministry to many people in that country.

In Psalm 55:22, God tells us to "*cast* [or roll] *your burden on the Lord* [don't keep talking about it], *and He shall sustain you.*" Because putting the truth of Psalm 37:5 into action is such an integral part of my life, with such wonderful results, I am going to share another story with you. Hopefully you will be inspired and motivated to apply God's Word to your own life when the inevitable difficult circumstances arise.

Don Stephens was a prominent young leader in Y.W.A.M. (Youth With A Mission) at the time of the events I will be sharing. He and I had been teaching in Egypt for a week, using interpreters, to a group of university students who were keen to learn about God's character and ways, in order to make Him known. It was a vital and rewarding time spiritually. We then needed to go on to Lausanne, Switzerland, to meet up with our spouses. Upon diligently seeking for God's specific directions as to when we were to fly out of Cairo, God had spoken to us from His Word that it was to be on Sunday afternoon.

The conference in Egypt was held in Alexandria, but the airport to leave Egypt was in Cairo. Our frequent attempts to book our flight out of Cairo failed because all the phone communications between Alexandria and Cairo were out of order. We left Alexandria for the two-and-a-half-hour train ride to Cairo, trusting God to get us flight reservations on arrival.

In my daily Bible reading on the train, God had quickened to me Psalm 9:10: "*Those who know Your name will put their trust in You; for You, Lord, have not forsaken those who seek You.*" We took a taxi to the airport in faith, only to be told on arrival, "There's no way you can get on the only flight into Switzerland today. It's fully booked and there are eight people already on the waiting list ahead of you." We smiled and said we would wait. I remembered that God had encouraged me from His word that He would come through, as we had sought Him for directions, and as long as we trusted Him. The easiest way to trust Him was to go through the steps outlined in Psalm 37:5. "Throw" the situation at Him and, because of who He is, believe that He catches everyone involved and then goes into action to solve the problem. We did just that and waited in faith.

At the last minute when everyone with tickets had boarded the plane, without any explanation about the other people ahead of us on the waiting list, the agent told us to get on board and handed us our tickets. There wasn't one seat left after we had boarded that plane and taken ours.

That first plane only took us as far as Athens, Greece. We had to get another plane to Zurich, Switzerland. When we arrived in Athens, we found that our plane to Zurich was already out on the tarmac with all the passengers on board and *the aircraft door was closed.* The airport officials stated, "There's no way you can get on board that plane. You're far too late." After much silent prayer, which included committing or "throwing" the airline personnel at God, as instructed in Psalm 37:5, and trusting Him to act, along with persuasive words from both Don and me, the unthinkable happened. The SwissAir agent suddenly reversed his previous decision, ordered a special car for us, and the driver took us out to the plane at breakneck speed, where they opened the plane door and let us on.

When we got to Zurich, exactly the same scene greeted us. The travel agent who wrote out our tickets in Cairo hadn't left enough time between plane changes. So at Zurich the officials said, "Your plane to Geneva is ready to leave. There's absolutely *no way* you can get on now."

Well, we'd heard that story twice before that day!! After more silent prayer, when we thanked God in faith that He would make a way, placing the airline officials firmly in His hands, we explained in as firm and as gracious a way possible that it was imperative that we get on that flight. Then God kicked into action. Suddenly, we were told to run to the plane while the agent phoned "the gate" (the last stop to the plane) and told them to delay it. We tore through the airport, and again just made it!!

It was an incredible day of seeing God fulfill what I have believed and taught for years. God will always make a way for those who will believe and obey. For those who will commit, trust, and fully believe, He will act as He promises in Psalm 37:5. (Our luggage caught up with us the next morning.)

I have found these sorts of circumstances to be exhilarating. It's a wonderful adventure seeing the living God actively involved in the affairs of His children who seek to know His specific directions and then, against all odds, continue to believe Him to fulfill what He has spoken.

It's obviously not *what* we know; it's *Who* we know. The creator and sustainer of the universe, King God, has a million ways we haven't heard of or thought of to make a way where there is no way for any of His kids who are on His business, in a fix, and are simple enough to believe that His Word works.

Why don't you put this book down and right now present to God what or who it is you're worrying about, represented by some object you can throw? Take a measured look at His character as I've described Him in the previous story, and then throw your problem at God and believe He's the greatest catcher and action-taker. Then laugh out loud and praise Him that He's working. It may not be immediately as in my two illustrations. Many times I've had to wait. But one thing you can count on is that He will act in His way and time if your deepest desire is for Him to get the greatest glory when He does.

The Test of Timing

This test is inevitable and can come in different forms. We'll now look at some of them and hopefully be enlightened and encouraged. In the process of writing this book, I was arrested in my daily Bible reading in John 6:15-21 with Jesus putting His disciples through the timing test. It starts in verse 14, right after the feeding of about 5,000 men, plus women and children. The disciples are convinced that Jesus is the real deal whom Moses prophesied about in Deuteronomy 18:15, and in presumption are ready to set up Jesus as King to rule over His earthly Kingdom.

Inherent in this bright idea of "eager beavers" is the fact that the cross and its eternal implications would be avoided. The idea sounds ingenious, but it would have fully cooperated with Jesus' greatest opposing party, the devil. To bypass this overtly wrong suggestion, Jesus took off smartly to His favorite hideout up in the mountain, alone with His favorite partner, the Father. The disciples hadn't a clue on God's timing and purpose for their lives, and often we have as little understanding as they did and, consequently, we flail around in confusion, unbelief, and perplexity.

The second stage of the disciples missing the timing test comes in John 6:17. The disciples had gotten into a boat and were rowing toward Capernaum, *"And it was already dark, and Jesus had not come to them."* It was bad enough that Jesus didn't buy their idea of promoting Him (and them) and getting on with what they perceived was what their following Him was all about, but now their elusive leader disappears. And they need Him. And it's dark. Sound familiar?

We don't know what's going on and we're puzzled that things are not adding up as they used to in our walk with the

Lord. Circumstances have gotten difficult and although previously we've been given promises by God about our future lives, they seem hollow and somehow we feel we're in the dark and we can't feel or hear Jesus like we used to. In fact, He seems to have disappeared from our scene altogether. We may cry out like David, who felt the same way, *"Do not forsake me, O Lord; O my God, be not far from me! Make haste to help me, O Lord, my salvation!"* (Psalm 38:21-22).

Back to the disciples. In John 6:18 we're told that everything got worse...*much* worse. The waves of the sea got higher and more menacing and a ferocious wind was roaring. *Still no Jesus.* By now, they're not only frightened (it's so dark), but they're exhausted from having rowed for three or four miles, wondering if they'll have the strength to make it to land.

The burning question is: Where in the world is Jesus, when we're this desperate for the help that only He can give? We're tempted to think: Has He forgotten our address? Is He napping or on overload? Doesn't He know what's going on? If He does, why doesn't He show up? Doesn't He care? Verses of Scripture seem to mock us by saying things like: *"Call upon Me in the day of trouble; I will deliver you"* (Psalm 50:15). We've done that. So we bleat out, or yell, one more time according to our strength levels, "Jesus help. Have mercy on me," remembering that's what did it for blind Bartimaeus.

Back to the disciples. Breakthrough! John 6:19 says that the disciples saw Jesus walking on the sea, coming toward their boat. They were in awe. Their fear for survival turned into the fear of the Lord as the Light of the world showed up at their darkest hour physically, mentally, and emotionally, and pierced the darkness by calmly announcing His presence and telling them to relax. If that weren't enough, they then experienced the "spacey" miracle of being supernaturally transported to where they wanted to land—without moving an oar!

What is Jesus saying to us through all this?

- God is always in control.
- He is never too late.
- In order for us to pass the timing test, He chooses to show up far later than we would expect or desire.
- He always has an answer to our problems and knows exactly how and when to solve them.
- He wants us to come to the place where we experience the rest of faith in dark and difficult times, because we've taken the time to study His character, facet by facet from His Word. That revelation inevitably produces peace.

It's worth noting that Saul didn't pass this important test as a newly appointed leader. Samuel told Saul that he would return to him within seven days and offer up the sacrifices (see First Samuel). This was part of Samuel's ministry function, not Saul's. When Saul saw the enemy approaching and Samuel hadn't yet arrived on the seventh day, Saul offered up the sacrifices.

This act of presumption and disobedience manifested the following in Saul:

- His lack of the fear of the Lord,
- His lack of trust in God's character to come through at a time of need,
- His lack of confidence in Samuel's character to keep his word,
- His pride that he could bend the rules to fit his judgments in leadership.

When Samuel arrived, just in time, and addressed all the above, he was prompted by God to announce that the hand of God was lifted off Saul for leadership and given to a much younger man, David. What a price to pay for not passing the timing test!

It doesn't matter how dark the circumstances or how tempted we are to despair, Jesus has clearly stated that He will never leave us nor forsake us. Which means, He'll always come through in His way and time…if we will call, trust, and obey!

Since July 1971, Jim and I have been unsalaried missionaries with Youth With A Mission. This organization doesn't pay wages, so we live entirely by faith. This gives God countless opportunities to prove Himself faithful, and on time, as we have lived through the numerous times He has tested us financially. I'll share just one of them here.

Jim and I were obeying God's directions to go and minister overseas, a normal part of our lives' ministry to the nations. As missionaries, we have spent very little time praying for finances for ourselves. We believe that if we focus on the advice in Matthew 6:33 and are "seeking first God's Kingdom" (making His interests and priorities our priorities) and "His righteousness" (making sure there is no unrepented sin in our lives) that it is God's responsibility to provide the money for us to obey Him. To us, that's not complicated, but it means making sure at all times that we are fulfilling those conditions without compromise.

In that context we had booked and recently purchased our airline tickets with an itinerary to two other countries. As it approached the day to leave, Jim worked out our expenses compared with the money in our bank account to cover them. We were short exactly $2,200. We thanked God that, as He wasn't poor or mean, He would come through in His timing and way. We knew of no hindrances in our lives that would prevent His doing so. And we hadn't a clue in the world how He would do His thing.

On the morning that we were leaving to drive to the Los Angeles airport to go to our destination, Jim said to me, "I've just got time to go to the post office and check our mailbox before we take off." He was back in no time with a grin from ear to ear and halfway down his back. He showed me a check in an envelope from a dear woman in North Carolina, written out for exactly $2,200. No letter. No explanation. Just the exact amount of money we needed—*on time!* God's perfect time. And only God knew about our need. We hadn't needed it any sooner, as the full payment would have previously been put on our credit card.

I can honestly say that at no time were we concerned about that need being met. In fact, we were as relaxed as poached eggs. The reason is simple. I have thoroughly studied and meditated on the faithfulness of God from His Word. Above our kitchen table we have a wooden plaque with the words written in white, "*He will not fail you*" (Deuteronomy 31:8 RSV). I not only believe those words, but I'm convinced that God doesn't know how to fail. Faithfulness is an integral part of His character. Therefore, He would have to come "unglued" in order to fail. "*If we are faithless, He remains faithful; He cannot deny Himself*" (2 Timothy 2:13).

Faith comes not only from hearing God's Word, but more importantly by believing in the character of the One who wrote the Word. Under severe persecution, torture, and brainwashing, believers could understandably forget memorized Scriptures, and at times they have, but no man or devil or device can erase the knowledge of God's character. That's one reason why we should make it a way of life to study it (Him).

The Main Purposes of the Fire of God in Testing

It is of paramount importance that we understand the main purposes of the fire of God in testing. We need to ponder the purposes, asking God to give us His perspective on their importance, and believe and thank Him that He will. I am now going to enumerate them.

The main purposes of the fire of God in testing are:

- To see whether we love the Lord our God with all our heart, soul, mind, and strength, or whether there are idols in our lives.

- To see whether we will act and react according to what God says in His Word and pass the test, or disobey God's instructions and fail the test.

- To see whether or not we will choose to live the life of dependence on the Lord Jesus as Jesus depended on the Father when Jesus was on earth.

- For God to prove to us that the more difficult the tests, the greater His rewards and bonuses, since they are commensurate as we pass those tests by obedience to His Word.

- To see whether or not we want to enter into the fellowship of Christ's sufferings in order to know Him intimately.

- To make us more like Jesus. As Romans 8:29 says, *"He also predestined [us] to be conformed to the image of His Son."*

- To bring glory to the Lord Jesus. *"That in all things God may be glorified through Jesus Christ"* (1 Peter 4:11).

- To give us further opportunities of proving the faithfulness of God, as we do our part to believe His Word and obey Him. Deuteronomy 7:9 says, *"Therefore know that the Lord your God, He is God, the faithful God who keeps covenant and mercy for a thousand generations with those who love Him and keep His commandments."* And John 15:7 says, *"If you abide in Me, and My words abide in you, you will ask what you desire, and it shall be done for you."*

- To bring us into a more intimate relationship with the Lord Jesus and have a deeper love for Him. John 14:21 says, *"He who has My commandments and keeps them, it is he who loves Me. And he who loves Me will be loved by My Father, and I will love him and manifest Myself to him."*

- To have a greater understanding of God's ways. Jeremiah 11:20 says, *"But, O Lord of hosts, You who judge righteously, testing the mind and the heart, let me see Your vengeance on them, for to You I have revealed my cause."*

- To receive the blessings that come from believing God's Word and obeying Him regardless of the circumstances. Deuteronomy 28:2 says, *"And all these blessings shall come upon you and overtake you, because you obey the voice of the Lord your God."*

- For God and us to see what level of humility is in our hearts in relation to obeying Him. Deuteronomy 8:2 says, *"The Lord your God led you all the way these forty years in the wilderness, to humble you and test you, to know what was in your heart, whether you would keep His commandments or not."*

- For God and us to see whether we fear God, or men, or satanic forces when they tempt us to sin. Genesis 22:12 says, *"Do not lay your hand upon the lad, or do anything to him; for now I know that you fear God, since you have not withheld your son, your only son, from Me."* Exodus 20:20 says, *"Do not fear; for God has come to test you, and that His fear may be before you, so that you may not sin."*

- To prove to God the extent of our love for Him through our obedience to Him regardless of the cost. Deuteronomy 13:3 says, *"For the Lord your God is testing you to know whether you love the Lord your God with all your heart and with all your soul."* John 14:15 says, *"If you love Me, keep My commandments."*

- For God and us to know our heart's motivation, about whether we live and speak to please men or God. First Thessalonians 2:4 (RSV) says, *"So we speak, not to please men, but to please God who tests our hearts."*
- Whether God can trust us with more privileges or responsibilities in relation to the extension of His Kingdom, both here on earth, and in eternity. Revelation 2:26 says, *"And he who overcomes, and keeps My works until the end, to him I will give power over the nations."*
- To see whether we will embrace the sovereignty of God when in the greatest test, the perplexity test. When God withholds all understanding of His purposes prolonged during suffering, and may at the same time cease speaking to us for a season, will we accept the truth from Romans 11:33 that at all times, *"His ways* [are] *past finding out"*? Will we rest in faith and peace of mind and heart that *"as for God, His way is perfect"* (Psalm 18:30), when 2+2 seems to make 47 most of the time?
- God tests us to see whether we will believe in His character even when we cannot understand His ways, having studied every aspect of it from His Word.
- Is it okay with us if we have to wait until we get to Heaven to have our deepest questions answered? Will we rest in the fact that Jesus said in John 13:7, *"What I am doing you do not understand now, but you will know after this"*?

God, in His flawless character, sets up tests basically to see how serious we are in wanting to know Him in order to make Him known.

In my *Resource Guide*, which is available from Youth With A Mission, Los Angeles, the reader is able to see and then order a three-part audiotape series (JD 14, JD 15, JD 16) on the subject of "The Testing of God's Children." Through the tapes I offer more information about how to recognize the tests and how to react to them according to the Bible. It is a more comprehensive teaching on this subject, revealing 21 tests. The *Resource Guide* gives all the information needed for ordering the tapes. To obtain a *Resource Guide*, please contact:

Youth With A Mission
11141 Osborne Street
Lake View Terrace, CA 91342, USA
Phone (818) 896-2755, FAX (818) 897-6738
E-mail: ywamla@compuserve.com

SECTION TWO

THE FIRE OF GOD IN POWER

In Job 26, we find a list of vivid examples of God's power as the creator and sustainer of the universe. For instance, *"He stretches out the north over empty space; He hangs the earth on nothing"* (verse 7), and *"The pillars of heaven tremble, and are astonished* [or "aghast," NIV] *at His rebuke. He stirs up the sea with His power, and by His understanding He breaks up the storm"* (verses 11-12). *"By His breath the skies became fair"* (verse 13, NIV).

Then Job makes this statement in verse 14: *"Indeed these are the mere edges of His ways, and how small a whisper we hear of Him! But the thunder of His power who can understand?"* The word *thunder* here means "to cause to roar." In Job 37:1, Elihu tries to explain his reaction to this kind of powerful roar by saying *"My heart trembles, and leaps from its place."* It's a majestic voice that roars and thunders.

The Thunder of God's Power

One of the most intense displays of the fire of God in power recorded in the Bible is in Exodus 19. God told Moses to tell the people to consecrate themselves for two days in preparation for an encounter with Him on the third day at the foot of Mount Sinai. He gave strict instructions for no one to go up the mountain or even touch its base. To violate this command meant death at the hand of God (see Exodus 19:12).

A loud trumpet sound was the cue to assemble together. This was a prelude to the giving of the Ten Commandments outlined in Exodus 20. I guess this was one of God's ways of getting the people to take Him seriously. With precision timing, on the morning of the third day, the big action started. The Creator of the universe unleashed enough of His raw power that *"all the people who were in the camp trembled"* (Exodus 19:16). Little wonder!

They saw and heard "thunderings and lightnings" as Mount Sinai became a raging inferno with smoke billowing everywhere. At the same time the whole mountain quaked violently and the trumpet sound became louder and louder. Add to that scenario, they heard God's audible voice booming out of the *"blackness and darkness and tempest"* (Hebrews 12:18).

Although Moses was well used to having fiery encounters with the great "I AM," this one scared him spitless. That's my paraphrase of Hebrews 12:21: *"And so terrifying was the sight that Moses said, 'I am exceedingly afraid and trembling.'"*

God spoke to Moses, calling him to visit with Him on the top of that flaming mountain, and He didn't say He would turn down the thermostat. I'd say that was the ultimate trip of a person being taken out of his comfort zone, wouldn't you? Don't ever underestimate the spiritual ambition of this man, Moses. He wanted to know God and was prepared to obey Him in doing so, even if it meant being burned to a crisp in the process! Don't think that's an exaggeration, because God commanded Moses—before he made the trip up the mountain—to warn the priests and the people not to attempt to get too close to Him for that very reason (see Exodus 19:21,24).

The children of Israel couldn't bear to hear the loud voice of God speaking to them directly in that setting. They opted for the voice of a man. Whereas, the Bible says Moses went toward God in the thick darkness. How desperate are we for intimate friendship with God? I would rather be close to God in the darkest circumstances of life than be with the crowd in the seeming safety of their comfort zones. The safest place at all times is under the shadow of God's wings, regardless of the temperature. And remember, Jesus is *"the light of the world"* and *"in Him is no darkness at all"* (John 8:12; 1 John 1:5). So the nearer we are to Him, the more light we'll experience. He promises us that His Word is a lamp to our feet and a light to our path (see Psalm 119:105).

Have you ever thought about God's miraculous protection that Moses must have experienced for him to have made it through that inferno to keep his appointment with the Fire-Maker that day? I can imagine Daniel's three Hebrew friends comparing notes with Moses when they made it to Heaven. Talk about the fire of God's power of protection! Those troopers must have the ultimate stories!

When God wanted to identify the supremacy of His Being to a nation, He chose to demonstrate it by fire falling from Heaven and consuming water-saturated wood (see 1 Kings 18:20-38). When God wanted to display the limitlessness of His power to show up the powerlessness of His enemies, He chose a man named Elijah to be His ambassador and spokesman who was impressed only with the might and majesty of the One who had planned the showdown. The winner of the contest on Mount Carmel was to be proven by the truth of the challenge, "The God who answers by fire, He is God."

Our God is "a consuming fire" (Deuteronomy 4:24; Hebrews 12:29), which means that fire is part of the very essence of His personhood. So, all He has to do is show up and choose to put that part of Himself on display. To the opposing party, it's hardly a contest. The outcome is determined before the show starts.

One of the most pathetic accounts of mankind's attempts of challenging the fire of God's power is reading about the prophets of Baal calling on the name of their god from morning till midday, saying, *"O Baal, hear us"* (1 Kings 18:26). When he didn't show up with fire, the prophets of Baal *"cut themselves...with knives and lances, until the blood gushed out on them"* (1 Kings 18:28). Then they spent all afternoon supposedly prophesying that the action would surely come. Now, that's a description of the determination and despair that comes from total disillusionment. That's when God loves to take center stage. He answered a brief, two-sentence prayer from His fearless prophet, and *"the fire of the Lord fell and consumed the burnt sacrifice, and the wood and the stones and the dust, and it licked up the water that was in the trench"* (1 Kings 18:38).

We all know that water is used to quench fire, but when the fire of God's power is unleashed, the reverse takes place and the fire consumes the water. Now that's God power! It is no wonder that when all the people saw this phenomenon from headquarters Heaven they cried out, *"The Lord, He is God! The Lord, He is God"* (1 Kings 18:39). How embarrassing a defeat for the opposition, and what a victory for the undefeated champion, God Almighty!

Then Elijah finished the showdown by executing the 450 prophets of Baal plus 400 prophets of Asherah. That's 950

men. I'm impressed with this obvious display of incredible supernatural strength. But I'm much more impressed with the mega-
power that emanates from the One, "[Who] *looks on the earth, and
it trembles; He touches the hills, and they smoke*" (Psalm 104:32).

God's Mega-Power

Now listen to the prophet Micah as he describes what it's like
when God flexes His muscles. "*For behold, the Lord is coming out
of His place; He will come down and tread on the high places of
the earth. The mountains will melt under Him, and the valleys will
split like wax before the fire, like waters poured down a steep
place*" (Micah 1:3-4). Think about that for raw power.

Perhaps one of the reasons why unbelief is so rampant in
those who profess to be followers of the Lord Jesus is because
they have never taken the time to study the biblical descriptions
of God's awesome power in action, in whichever form it may be
manifest.

The prophet Nahum announced to the people of Nineveh, a
hundred years after God had demonstrated His mercy by sparing it
from judgment, that "*the Lord is slow to anger and great in power,
and will not at all acquit the wicked*" (Nahum 1:3).

The Assyrians had forgotten their previous revival and true
spiritual awakening and had turned back to their former sins of
violence and idolatry. Nahum proclaims to them the downfall of
the same city as he describes how God's power will be manifest:
"*The mountains quake before Him, the hills melt, and the earth
heaves at His presence, yes, the world and all who dwell in it.
Who can stand before His indignation? And who can endure the
fierceness of His anger? His fury is poured out like fire, and the
rocks are thrown down by Him*" (Nahum 1:5-6).

Trembling at God's Presence

This is a description of mountains moving, shaking, and melting at God's presence, while the whole planet is traumatized. That means He doesn't have to do anything but show up and the most awesome displays of the fire of God's power are activated. God calls us to tremble before Him as we pause to consider His creative power in doing the absolutely impossible-to-man things at times of their desperate need. *"Tremble, O earth, at the presence of the Lord…who turned the rock into a pool of water, the flint into a fountain of waters"* (Psalm 114:7-8).

The impossible-to-man doesn't impress, intimidate, faze, or challenge God. The fire of God's power and purposes in the affairs of mankind can't be stopped. At the same time God calls us to tremble at His presence, in the fear of the Lord, as we ponder His awesome control over the elements He created. *"'Do you not fear Me?' says the Lord. 'Will you not tremble at My presence, who have placed the sand as the bound of the sea, by a perpetual decree, that it cannot pass beyond it?'"*(Jer. 5:22).

I believe God's Word and take it, and Him, seriously. Here's an illustration. At a recent combined churches retreat, on a Saturday night after I had given the message on "The Justice of God," I gave an opportunity for the audience to respond openly. Varied moves of God's Spirit followed, meeting deep needs of individuals, after which God directed me to share two Scriptures: Psalm 99:1, *"The Lord reigns; let the peoples tremble!"* and Ezra 9:4, *"Then everyone who trembled at the words of the God of Israel assembled to me [Ezra]…."*

Then the Holy Spirit directed me to call everyone to stand at full attention as we would if an earthly monarch were entering the room. We did this with our eyes closed for an extended time, while focusing in worship, in total silence, solely on God's majestic splendor, pristine purity, and blazing glory.

This resulted in a visitation of the Lord's awesome presence, which was manifest in a number of different ways to His waiting people. Several, including the retreat leader, had a vision of the Lord Jesus in a long robe, walking between the rows of people while His robe brushed up against each person. It was in contrast to the woman in the Bible who had to press through the crowds in order to touch the hem of Jesus' robe. How gracious and merciful Jesus is! According to the many meaningful, wonderful testimonies that followed, it was truly a life-changing experience. All glory to the King!

During the silent worship time, the Holy Spirit came upon my body with strong trembling from my head and shoulders, through my arms and hands, for at least 15 minutes. In general, the Body of Christ experiences very little of what it means to tremble in the presence of our awesome God. Could that be because we know so little of the discipline of silent, focused worship?

In the midst of all the celestial drama and pageantry of Heaven, including untold multitudes of praising saints who are doing so without a vestige of restraint, an unusual thing will take place. Revelation 8:1 tells us there will be total silence in Heaven for about half an hour. For those who never engaged themselves in silent worship on earth, it will be a shocking experience, possibly unnerving. We mortals have become so accustomed to noise and action when we meet together that most are uncomfortable when waiting in silence before God.

The Explosive Effects of the Gospel

The fire of God's power is manifest in many different ways. But none more effectively than when the Word of God describes the explosive effect of the gospel when presented in the power of the Holy Spirit through surrendered, clean vessels to needy souls. The apostle Paul said, *"The gospel...is the power* [dynamite] *of God to salvation for everyone who believes..."* (Romans 1:16).

In a recent published report of some of the workings of the Holy Spirit in South Asia, in relation to the spreading of the gospel, I have read about the fire of God's power blasting through the Islamic religion in unprecedented proportions. For many years, The JESUS Film, produced by Campus Crusade for Christ International, has been mightily used of God to bring multiplied millions to Christ and to plant churches. The miraculous has been repeatedly and vividly demonstrated. The film has been translated into over 800 languages, and to date, there are at least 195,198,152 recorded decisions of people signifying their commitment of life to Christ. There are also many more that are unrecorded. The following is a report from Paul Eshleman, the former Director of The JESUS Film Project.

The year was 1995, in a troubled country of North Africa. A horrendous civil war had left millions dead, injured, mutilated or displaced. Large numbers of refugees had fled for their lives to the capital city. There they were rounded up in trucks, like cattle, and transported to large refugee camps in the north. Left to languish in the desert, they were told, "You will become Muslim here, or die." The refugees named their camp **"They Abandoned Us."**

While some organizations were helping with humanitarian aid, a JESUS film team sought also to meet their deepest spiritual needs. They made the difficult journey by jeep through the open and largely roadless desert. The team arrived at 4:30 in the afternoon and proceeded to set up their equipment. Word spread that something big was happening. The people began to gather around the single screen and projector.

By the time the first reel of the JESUS film finished there were 3,000 refugees sitting on both sides of the screen. The second reel started. People continued to stream in until there were 6,000 people watching a film that spoke to them in their mother tongue.

Their hearts were touched by the incomparable love of Jesus. When He spoke, His words—the Word of God— reached down deep into their souls. With every miracle they cheered. Never had they experienced anything like this. As He was beaten and crucified, they wept. When He returned from the dead, they rose to their feet together with a shout and began tapping one another on the shoulder, a sign of joy. At the conclusion of the film, the team leader went to the microphone and again explained the gospel. He then asked: "Now, who wants to receive Jesus as Lord and Savior?"

An estimated 3,000 people (half the number of those present) trusted Jesus that night. God's Spirit moved powerfully! Then the follow-up began where they were taught the Scriptures and who Jesus really is, God Himself. The refugees soon renamed their camp "**They Adopted Us.**"

Next they memorized the Scriptures and were taught how to impart their faith to others. As a result, they again renamed the camp, "**They Are Sending Us,**" because they began going out to other camps sharing Christ, and helping to show JESUS. This was God's doing!

Six years earlier, when the JESUS film was first used in this country, there were only three workers—one staff member and two volunteers. Now there are 150 full-time, national staff. Ten million people have viewed

JESUS in this country and many thousands have indicated their decisions. Each year, 3000 new believers
attend an extensive, 100-hour training and discipleship
course. Ten churches are planted every month and most
of the pastors are graduates from the course!

Is this not all cause for celebration and praise? From my
heart, I agree with the Apostle Paul "....to the only God
our Savior be glory, majesty, power and authority,
through Jesus Christ our Lord, before all ages, now and
forever! Amen." (Jude, verse 25, NIV)

This concludes Paul Eshleman's report.[1]

The media is playing a highly significant role. Christian television programs aired by the Christian Broadcasting Network have
generated approximately 200,000 letters from the Middle East
region. In a follow-up survey, 10 percent of the respondents from
Uzbekistan and 23 percent from Kazakhstan indicated that they
had prayed to ask Jesus into their hearts. This indicates, at the very
least, a significant openness to the gospel and, at the most, that
many hundreds of thousands of Central Asian Muslims have
already reached out for salvation.

Trans World Radio and F.E.B.C. annually receive 500,000 lis-
tener letters. The report I read said that "together with the various
literature saturation efforts that are currently under way, these
gospel programs are responsible for exposing tens of millions of
un-reached Indians to the claims of Christ each year."[2]

However, it is a film on the life of Christ that has proven to be
the most effective means of spreading the gospel in India. The
film is titled *Daya Sagar*—meaning "Oceans of Mercy." It was
produced in the 1970s by a leading Hindu filmmaker, Vijay Chan-
dar, who has since become a Christian evangelist. The film has
now been dubbed into six Indian languages and is shown almost
daily. According to an Indian mission leader, it has become the

single most effective tool to gain entrance into villages, schools, and communities that otherwise would never allow any kind of gospel work.

John Gilman, the founder of Dayspring International who distributes this film, has stated that over 80,000,000 people in India have seen it and over 6,000,000 have accepted Christ as Savior, and thousands of churches have been established. The remarkable story surrounding this film can be read in John Gilman's book, *They're Killing an Innocent Man*, published by Dayspring International. This is the source of the above information.

Perhaps one of the greatest recent blows to satan's kingdom and the advancement of Christ's Kingdom has come through the unprecedented numbers of people worldwide who have seen and been spiritually impacted by Mel Gibson's film, *The Passion of Christ*. It vividly portrays the Lord Jesus' agonizing hours before and during the crucifixion. I heard and saw a TV interview with a man who had interviewed over 70,000 people who had testified to God's transforming power operating in their lives as a direct result of seeing this movie made in Hollywood. By the time this book is published that number will have greatly increased.

The Transforming Fire of God's Power

I am impressed with the dynamite of God's transforming power that works in peoples' lives when they surrender themselves to the timeless One who existed before the universe was spoken into existence: God Almighty, my wonderful Savior, my Lord and Master, my closest companion, the lover of my soul, the only one who can totally fulfill me—Jesus, beautiful, precious Jesus. "*Yes, he is altogether lovely. This is my beloved, and this is my friend*" (Song of Solomon 5:16). More than that, "*I am my beloved's, and his desire is toward me*" (Song of Solomon 7:10).

You, dear reader, can have that exact same tender testimony if you will come to Him just as you are. Don't try to be religious. Just be real. Tell the Lord Jesus that you're through with trying to run your own life. Tell Him that you believe He came to this earth as the Son of God and took the punishment for your sins when He died on the cross. Thank Him for that supreme act of unconditional love. Invite Him to come into your heart and life and receive Him by faith. Ask Him to take over completely as you make Him your Lord and master, the boss.

When we give everything of ourselves to the Lord without reserve—our past, present, and future—He makes all of Himself totally available to us. What a fantastic exchange! It's an incredible deal. What a relief that the One who made the universe and is in control of it, now takes over total responsibility for our lives when we come to Him in childlike trust.

I gave my life over to the Lord Jesus when I was five years of age, and I have proved over the ensuing decades that I don't have a clue what is best for me. The most unnerving thing I could think of would be if I had the responsibility of running my own life. The greatest comfort is having the assurance that my life is in the hands of my Creator, *Father God*; my Savior and Redeemer, the *Lord Jesus*; and my Guide, Comforter, and Enabler, the *Holy Spirit*—three in equal authority but different in function: the Triune God.

Jesus said in John 14:6 that He is "the way, the truth, and the life," and that no one comes to God the Father except through Him. So, for God to become our Father, not just our Creator, we must have a personal encounter with the Lord Jesus, as I've been explaining. When Jesus was talking to a Jewish Rabbi, He explained that it was the equivalent of being born all over again; only this time it's a spiritual birth. You become God's child—part of His family—through making His Son, the

Lord Jesus Christ, your Savior and Lord. This then is your pass-
port into Heaven where you experience eternal life. *"He who
has the Son has life; he who does not have the Son of God does
not have life"* (1 John 5:12).

The amazing dynamite of God's transforming power to
change us from self-focused people into God-and-other-people-
focused people is something that only comes through letting the
living Lord Jesus become the center of our lives. That's living. All
else is merely existing.

Now, let us look at the fire of God's power to overcome the
powers of darkness. God's Word says, *"He* [the Lord Jesus] *who
is in you is greater than he* [satan] *who is in the world"* (1 John
4:4 RSV). So we shouldn't be surprised at hearing stories of
great triumphs over the devil. Remember, our Commander-in-
Chief has never lost a battle. He's El Shaddai, God Almighty.
He's the ruling, reigning Monarch of the universe. King God!

David Piper was a young man with a strong Christian her-
itage who had chosen to rebel against the truth about God's compelling love and His plans for David's life. As a result of going his
own way, he became heavily addicted to alcohol and drugs,
became a criminal, and was imprisoned. In desperation to become
free from the hellish bondage to the worst drugs, he made a move
toward the Lord Jesus and sought help from spiritual leaders who
ministered to him. This brought partial release, but he suc-
cumbed to the first temptation by satanic forces and went right
back to the drugs.

In telling the story of his life, David explains that he was
seeking deliverance by coming to the Lord Jesus, but he was not
seeking the Lord for Himself. He wanted what the Lord could do
for him, but was not prepared to submit to His control—nor was
he prepared to humble himself before others and acknowledge the
truth about his failure.

Although he cried out to God for deliverance on his own for a month, he had no sense of God's presence and thought God had abandoned him. However, God had a plan, and he used David's godly grandmother to make it work. She asked David to drive her and some of their other elderly Christian relatives to a Benny Hinn Crusade. It was 260 miles from where they lived. David didn't want to go, but reluctantly agreed, feeling that if he didn't come to God in all honesty and real repentance, this could be his last chance.

At the crusade in Orlando, Florida, on the first night as the worship began, David began to seek God with all his heart, for Himself and for His presence. On the second day of the Crusade, during the worship time, David came under deep conviction of his rebellion against God's plan for his life. He openly wept in sincere repentance, and for the first time, surrendered his life completely to God, sensing the Lord's presence all around him.

After the worship finished and Pastor Benny started preaching, while David was still weeping and repenting before God, his body trembled all over and then numbness moved from his fingertips to his elbows. He became aware of Christ's manifest presence as never before. David's whole being was experiencing some of the fire of God's power and at the same time he was sensing the fire of God's glory. Nearing the end of the service, David responded to the urging of the Holy Spirit to go down to the front of the platform, in response to Benny Hinn's invitation for those who were called of God into full-time ministry, to come forward for prayer.

To David's shock and amazement, suddenly Benny Hinn looked straight at him and said, "Young man, you in the brown shirt, come up here." When David got onto the platform, Pastor Benny pointed to him and said, "Father, anoint him." In David's own words this is what followed.

*Immediately I felt the fire of God flow into me like a hot,
burning liquid. It flowed down my throat and into my
stomach, and on settling there, it exploded inside of me
like a stick of dynamite. I have never felt anything like it
before, nor have I known anything like it since. Instantly,
I was delivered from my addictions. All my sensory
memories of the drugs, alcohol and tobacco were gone.
I left the service that day and could not tell you what a
glass of beer tasted like. It was as though I never had
one. I couldn't remember the taste of a cigarette or any
of the feelings associated with my drug use. God's
anointing had broken the yoke with which these things
had bound me. The Lord had released my deliverance
because I had finally come to Him in repentance and
brokenness, seeking Him and only Him.
My life would change from that point onward. I couldn't
stand to be around the crowd I had been with. I couldn't
turn on the television set and watch shows I had always
watched. God had burned the desire for those things
right out of me and placed inside of me a desire for Him
and for His ways. I couldn't get enough prayer. I could-
n't get enough worship time. Not only did the Lord set
me free from my bondages; He also filled me with a
hunger for Him like I had never known before.[3]*

David Piper has been a full-time evangelist for a number of
years, being greatly used of God in many nations, helping people
to give their lives totally to the Lordship of Jesus Christ.

Miraculous Intervention

I just love the way God describes Himself: searching all over
the world with His all-seeing eyes, seeking to find anyone on
planet Earth who is loyal to His character and who is in desperate
need of help, just so that He can demonstrate to them the fire of

His power! The fact is, God has the time of His life doing it. It's one of His favorite things. Check it out in Second Chronicles 16:9. What a fantastic God!

He never runs out of ideas of how to show up in the most horrendous and seemingly hopeless situations because He's ingenious in His creativity. He has at least five million ways of demonstrating the fire of His power that we've never heard of or thought of. So, why don't we wise up and give Him more opportunities to put Himself on display?

A group of Otomi believers in the village of San Nicholas in the Mezquital Valley of Mexico did just that. Because they had left the religious traditions of the Otomis and had become Christians, they faced increasing persecution, which led to the other villagers demanding that they leave. The believers settled on a bare hill on the other side of Ixmiquilpan, a place where no one else wanted to live.

One day, the Christians heard about a plan that was to be carried out that same night to exterminate them all. One of the women believers who had been there the longest went to every hut, urging the people to pray for help and to put their trust in God. She said, "Don't be afraid. God isn't dead!" Some were afraid to come into the open on top of the hill for fear of bullets from the ambush. But gradually, the trembling believers slowly assembled. In simple faith they pled for God's protection and for Him to somehow display His glory. In faith they went back to their huts and slept.

The next day, in the streets of Ixmiquilpan, people gathered in small groups, staring at the Christians and whispering among themselves. Gradually the story became known. Several hundred men, intent on exterminating every Christian and armed with dynamite and other weapons, had gathered the night before at the bottom of the hill. At a given signal, they started up toward the believers, when suddenly God turned on the fire of His power. To their horror they saw the whole hilltop was covered with a glaringly bright light, with the little church building in full view. They could see soldiers circling the hilltop, all holding guns and all ready to fire. Then trumpets began playing loudly.

The angry mob reported the next day that they couldn't get up the hill because they couldn't pass the "guards." Every Christian was spared from death. They knew that our miracle-working God had spotted them when He was looking for someone to whom He could display His glory by the fire of His power at a time of desperate need. They proved that powerful promise in Psalm 34:7: *"The angel of the Lord encamps all around those who fear Him, and* [He] *delivers them."*

At one point it had seemed that the little Otomi congregation might be snuffed out in a single night. But now there are some 5,000 believers scattered in 54 village congregations who have the New Testament translated and printed in their own Otomi language through the Wycliffe Bible Translators.

Jesus said, *"I will build My church, and the gates of* [hell] *shall not prevail against it"* (Matthew 16:18). We must only and always be impressed with the One who said these words—never the one who challenges them.

THE FIRE OF GOD TO PURIFY

I can imagine some people questioning the validity of linking the fire of God in purifying with His tender love. I can imagine others wanting to avoid reading this section because we all know that getting too close to fire is very painful, and many are in enough pain now, thank you.

I can recall, on a couple of occasions when individuals came up to me after my Bible teaching and told me that having once heard me speak they decided they never wanted to hear me again. The messages were too convicting. My reaction was always to smile and tell them that was their prerogative and to thank them for their honesty. Obviously, between their initial reaction and these conversations they had decided to try me out again.

My heart longs for believers everywhere to understand that when we see our heavenly Bridegroom face to face, we'll see that His eyes not only burn with awesome holiness and shine with pristine purity, but they blaze with unfathomable love for us. Added to that, our magnificent Master has the strongest possible spiritual ambition for us to be like Him—in fact, to be conformed to His image. Wow! Is that really possible? Yes, because in Romans 8:29, He says so.

I realize this has already been emphasized, but we need to be continually reminded of the priority of God's purposes in our lives here on earth. It's all about being prepared to become the Bride of Christ at the marriage supper of the Lamb (see Ephesians 5:25-27). It's about preparation for the big long-haul of time called eternity.

Acts of God's Love

Now let's see how the tender, strongly ambitious love of God manifests itself, or Himself, in relation to purifying us.

Sin in any form is the most destructive force to the well-being of our minds, bodies, souls, and spirits. *"The wages of sin is death"* (Romans 6:23), the ultimate destruction. It is like a disease. Let's take cancer as an example. Ultimately, it is destructive if not removed. We realize when we go to the doctors for tests that they help us by giving us a correct diagnosis. Our very life can depend on it. When we realize we have the disease, we desperately want to be rid of it.

Wouldn't it be ridiculous to either avoid the doctors' ability to give us an accurate diagnosis of the disease, or resent them when they do; worse still, if we would do nothing about having it removed in the many ways that God has provided. It could be through medical science or a miracle healing directly through prayer, or through applying natural means, or a combination of any of these ways.

Following this analogy we can only conclude that God does us the greatest favor by convicting us of this most destructive force called sin. When we realize that He is equally motivated by His love and His holiness to bring conviction, we see it as one of the greatest ways He can bless us. Sin not only destroys us, but it separates us from the only one who can fulfill us. *"He disciplines us for our good, that we may share His holiness"* (Hebrews 12:10 RSV). *"I counsel you to buy from Me gold refined by fire, that you may be rich, and white garments to clothe you.... Those whom I love, I reprove and chasten; so be zealous and repent"* (Revelation 3:18-19 RSV).

As we cooperate with God through genuine repentance, which means a change of heart, mind, and life toward each sin, we experience the wonder of not only getting closer to the Maker and Sustainer of the universe but actually becoming more like Him. What a break!

My story is to say, as a way of life, "Dear Holy Spirit, bring on conviction of sin wherever and whenever needed in my life. I need that blessing—big time!!" It is promised: *"Blessed are the people who know the joyful sound! They walk, O Lord, in the light of Your countenance"* (Psalm 89:15).

In the early fifties, when I was earnestly seeking God to reveal to me the truths about the Holy Spirit, I asked a number of spiritual leaders to explain the meaning of the words *"and fire"* from the verse in Matthew 3:11 when John the Baptist said concerning Jesus, *"He will baptize you with the Holy Spirit and fire."*

None of those leaders gave me a satisfactory answer, so I continued to seek God for understanding. In His faithfulness He revealed to me that the explanation was in the following verse. Matthew 3:12 says, *"His winnowing fan is in His hand, and He will thoroughly clean out His threshing floor, and gather His wheat into the barn; but He will burn up the chaff with unquenchable fire."*

The light dawned that this fire of the Holy Spirit was to burn out the things in my life that were un-Christlike. This truth then explained to me why I immediately went through a time of humbling straight after I was initially filled with the Holy Spirit as commanded in Ephesians 5:18: *"Be filled with the Spirit."*

Repeatedly, I would either be convicted directly by the Holy Spirit over something in my life that was grieving Him, or God would cause others to correct me. It was a very painful but necessary experience in my spiritual growth. I didn't have the full understanding at that time that it was an act of God's love to bless me.

But I was beginning to understand that the depth of our worship to the One True God, the Father, Son, and Holy Spirit is in direct proportion to the revelation we have of His holiness. *"Holiness, without which no one will see the Lord"* (Hebrews 12:14).

In Second Corinthians 7:1 (RSV), Paul says, *"Let us cleanse ourselves from every defilement of body and spirit, and make holiness perfect in the fear of God."* An effective way I have found of obeying this injunction is to ask God to show me my heart as only He sees it.

Second Chronicles 6:30 says, *"You alone know the hearts of the sons of men."* The two root sins from which all other sins come are unbelief and pride. They are the two sins by which satan tempted Eve in the Garden of Eden. *"Has God indeed said?"*—Unbelief. *"You shall be as God"*—Pride. (See Genesis 3.)

During a regular prayer meeting held in our home with my husband and three evangelists, I was praying for lost souls in the city in which we lived, when I first asked God to "show me my heart as You see it." I wanted my motives to be pure as we were engaged in extensive evangelism. Immediately the Holy Spirit answered me by giving me a revelation of my heart as it related to bringing correction to others. He showed me that to some of the men in the room I had pointed out some small areas that needed correction in their lives while never having seen the need to apply the same correction to my own life. For 15 minutes or more, I sobbed my heart out to God in deep repentance as He showed me the pride of my heart and I acknowledged it openly. I was deeply changed by that experience.

The most life-changing method God instructed me to do in relation to Second Corinthians 7:1 (RSV), "[making] *holiness perfect in the fear of God*," was to make an in-depth Bible study on the fear of the Lord and apply it to every area of my life. According to Proverbs 8:13, "*The fear of the Lord is to hate evil.*" Simply put, it means to have a passion for holiness in thought, word, and deed and to hate sin in the same dimensions. The Word of God alone is the standard. (Much later, this subject became the basis of my first book, a best-seller, and now printed in 20 different languages.)

Prior to going on my first Bible teaching trip to seven nations, I was convicted by the Holy Spirit three times in one week of the sin of pride. In order to really repent of that sin, I realized I needed to see the *root* of pride in my heart. As only God can reveal that knowledge to me, I got in a room alone and with a desperate desire and faith asked God to reveal to me my heart as He alone knows it, and I fully believed that He would. Nothing happened.

I then remembered how Jacob wrestled with God before he became a changed man. So I asked God again for divine revelation of my heart and told Him three times that I wouldn't let Him go until I saw the root sin of pride. Absolutely nothing happened.

Then I thought of Moses who pled God's character to God when interceding on behalf of the children of Israel. So I tried again, telling God in desperation and faith, that because of His faithfulness and because He had started this conviction, He therefore needed to come through and complete the work He had started, quoting, "*He who has begun a good work in you will complete it*" (Philippians 1:6) and "*The Lord will perfect that which concerns me*" (Psalm 138:8). Like Jacob, I wrestled with God again and said, "I will not let You go. I will not let You go. I will not let You go."

Then it happened! I saw the mixed motives of my heart. Jim and I were heavily involved in the Teen Challenge ministry and other forms of personal and mass evangelism in and outside the spheres of our church. From time to time I would report to our pastor some of the results of the conversions that were taking place when the ministry was not connected with the church.

God revealed to me under the bright searchlight of the Holy Spirit's flame, that although I genuinely had a burden for lost souls and gave some of the glory to God, I was at the same time taking some of it for myself by hoping that the pastor would be impressed by my zeal. It was a horrifying discovery. Pride is so obnoxious. I sobbed my way to deep repentance of the sin God hates the most. Pride heads the list of seven things that are an abomination to God (see Proverbs 6:17-19).

Then the realization came to me that I was to humble myself and make restitution to my pastor by telling him exactly what God in His unending mercy had shown me. After waiting three days to get an interview, I obeyed God and was graciously received by an understanding man of God. That experience made an indelible imprint on my life and was part of the needed preparation for God's plan to send me out to the nations to teach His Word, over a three-month period. The truth of "*My glory I will not give to another*" (Isaiah 42:8) was indelibly burned into my spirit.

Purity and Power

I also learned that true brokenness before God and man is a powerful means of releasing the power of the Holy Spirit upon us. *"But on this one will I look* [the one who gets God's attention]: *on him who is poor and of a contrite spirit, and who trembles at My word"* (Isaiah 66:2). I was also greatly encouraged by noticing that the enabling power of the Holy Spirit to minister to others was in exact proportion to the level of purity I was experiencing. Purity and power became synonymous. *"This is what the Lord has said, 'I will show Myself holy among those who are near Me, and before all the people I will be glorified'"* (Leviticus 10:3 RSV).

How wonderfully kind of God to express His tender love to me through deep conviction of sin. This experience drew me much closer to Him and deepened my love for Him and understanding of Him. *"As many as I love, I rebuke and chasten"* (Revelation 3:19). *"No chastening seems to be joyful for the present, but painful; nevertheless, afterward it yields the peaceable fruit of righteousness to those who have been trained by it"* (Hebrews 12:11). I was learning to appreciate and cooperate with God's loving training program.

Many years later, during times of intense, prevailing prayer prior to a large international evangelistic outreach during the 1984 Olympic Games in Los Angeles, I was again crying out to God to reveal anything that would hinder the outpouring of His Spirit upon our city. Another painful but necessary milestone of conviction and humbling was the result, but with it God gave me understanding and further encouragement from Daniel 11:33-35: *"And those of the people who understand shall instruct many.... And some of those of understanding shall fall, to refine them, purify them, and make them white."*

I was getting greater revelation that part of God's personal, tender love for me was to affirm to me that by His grace to enable me to make right choices, He had produced a vessel who had a measure of His wisdom to instruct many from His Word. And because of that high privilege and responsibility, I needed a deeper level of refining and purifying through repentance of sin in order to be more like Him and therefore more useful. Great gratitude and far less pain accompanied this experience because I was proving that the benefits from repentance far outweighed the humbling involved. *"Blessed are the pure in heart, for they shall see God"* (Matthew 5:8).

Never resist the convicting fires of the Holy Spirit; embrace them and cooperate with God in true repentance, with gratitude that He is bringing you closer in relationship with Jesus and preparing you for greater usefulness in His Kingdom purposes. What immense privileges!!

I was intrigued to learn from a recently converted Persian believer that the god that the Persians worship is the god of fire, because they believe that fire is the greatest purifying force. Their respect to worship this force came from the fact that, to them, it was the greatest symbol of purity. That is not only interesting, but significant. I believe the depth of our worship to God is the extent of our understanding of His awesome holiness.

I can honestly say that the personal pain associated with the humbling of confession and repentance of sin is now almost nil, but is replaced by far more sorrow for having hurt my precious Lord, mixed with the joyous release of peace and the increased power of the Holy Spirit to minister Jesus' life to others.

This explains why my favorite speakers are always those who are used of God to bring the enormous blessing of conviction of sin wherever it's needed in my life. I also greatly appreciate those who have gone deeper in their experiences with God than I have and have a greater revelation of God's character and ways. Bring them on, God!

I was given the opportunity of having an increased awareness of what God's holiness is like when I received the following letter

from one of the students in Youth With A Mission who had listened to my teaching on "The Highway of Holiness" referred to
in Isaiah 35:8. I had taught at length on what it means to live in
the biblical standard of holiness in our thoughts, our words, and
in our deeds and that it is attainable in the power of the Holy
Spirit on a daily basis as we obey the Word of God. She wrote
to me as follows:

My name is Marie Rigotti; I am a French girl and I am
28 years old. I've been saved for 2 ½ years. I have been
through two YWAM training schools with outreaches in
Chile and Israel. In December, before I went to Chile, I
watched again your video message on "The Highway of
Holiness" during which time you read scriptures from
Revelation 1:12-16, describing the Lord.... I literally
had a picture, a vision of the Lord Jesus...indescribable.
Since that time I have had an even greater desire to
know Him more, and also the desire and passion for
holiness. I really do want to be as holy as He is!

Well, when I went to Chile in January, I was really desiring to know more about His holiness. This desire was
becoming so strong. I cannot even tell about it. One day,
in a meeting at the end of the outreach in Chile, I said to
God in my heart, "Lord, I want to see Your holiness."
And Joy, what an experience... the Lord revealed His
holiness to me!!!

I literally saw an intense, burning fire...it was intensively
[sic] white ...it was all light, not any kind of shadow in
it...the light reflected was so intense, so pure...it was like
(if I can give a good kind of description) a thousand of
thousands (maybe more) of "suns." I was there standing
by the holy and pure fire of God. I realized that God was
all pure and all holy: This is God's holiness, which is total
purity!! I also realized that I was not (yet!) as holy as He

is, but I know that I can be, because He said I could: "You
should be holy for I am holy."

I was standing right in front of Him in His holiness, but
it was less than a second (for me it seemed more than a
second), and I didn't want to leave His presence; it was
too wonderful. The Lord told me just this: "You cannot
stay too long, otherwise you would be burned yet
[sic]." Then the vision left. What a tremendous and
wonderful experience, Joy! God reveals Himself to
those who seek Him and want to know Him.... Why?
Because He is Just, Righteous and True.... And
because He never lies and always fulfills His promises.
Numbers 23:19 is truth! When God speaks about Himself it is always true, because He is the Truth, the Way
and the Life. Amen![4]

After reading that experience from someone who had only
been a Christian for two and a half years, I was deeply challenged.
God had rewarded that young believer with a vision of His white-
hot holiness because of the intensity of her desire to experience it.

I had taught the students that God would never set a standard
for us if it were not possible to attain it in His power and divine
enabling because He is just. That's why she was making the point
about God's character at the close of her letter. God rewarded that
young woman because of the diligence with which she sought
Him. How much do we really want to know Him?

Going Deeper

Now let's take a look at God giving us another invitation to
become more like Him by further cooperating with the fires of His
love, and to avoid the fire of His judgment. *"For thus says the
Lord... 'Break up your fallow ground, and do not sow among thorns.
Circumcise yourselves to the Lord, and take away the foreskins of*

your hearts...lest My fury come forth like fire, and burn so that no one can quench it, because of the evil of your doings'" (Jeremiah 4:3-4).

The Living Letters translation says it this way: *"Plow up the hardness of your hearts; otherwise the good seed will be wasted among the thorns. Cleanse your minds and hearts, not just your bodies, or else My anger will burn you to a crisp because of all your sins. And no one will be able to put the fire out."*

Plowing involves disruption of the status quo and uncomfortable change. We're reminded of Jesus' encouraging words in John 8:32 that *"you shall know the truth, and the truth shall make you free,"* but we also know that the truth often hurts before we experience the freedom.

Let's look at some of the agricultural reasons for plowing and then apply them spiritually so that we can obey God's injunctions here.

The first purpose for plowing is to get rid of the hardness of the soil. We can too easily develop a coldness of heart toward God, His people, or the unconverted. Therefore we need to maintain a vigilant watch over the condition of our hearts.

When we are really serious about having a spiritual heart transplant, we'll cry out to God with intensity and faith for the Holy Spirit to break our hearts over what breaks God's heart. We may have to have the supernatural revelation of our heart's condition as only God knows it before a permanent change takes place.

God tells us in Jeremiah 17:9 that *"the heart is deceitful above all things, and desperately wicked; who can know it?"* The answer is found in Second Chronicles 6:30. Only God knows it. The following story illustrates this truth again.

One time, when I was overseas on one of my many teaching ministry trips, I sensed the need for personal spiritual renewal, but

I had no knowledge of the area that needed the change. So, once again I sought the face of God in desperation and faith to give me a revelation of my heart, and I wrestled with Him like Jacob, as previously described in this section. It was an intense time of prevailing prayer. This time God required another spiritual leader to witness my search for truth, which was even more humbling.

The result was very surprising and shocking to me. I knew that God knew that I was a genuinely warm, loving wife to my husband Jim and a loving mother to our son John and our daughter Jill. But what I didn't know was that there was a very small part of my heart that was cold toward each of them, which manifested itself in different ways to each one. I acknowledged it to God with many tears and deep brokenness, and then to each one of them when I returned home. They all said they were entirely unaware of my need for repentance in this area but received me lovingly. I came to understand what the Psalmist prayed in Psalm 90:8, "You have set our iniquities before You, our secret [meaning unknown to us] sins in the light of Your countenance."

I was now also understanding at a deeper level what Paul was praying for his dear friends the Thessalonians. "*And may the Lord make you increase and abound in love to one another and to all, just as we do to you, so that He may establish your hearts blameless in holiness before our God and Father at the coming of our Lord Jesus Christ with all His saints*" (1 Thessalonians 3:12-13).

In the next two days following this time of brokenness before the Lord, while still away ministering, at times tears would involuntarily flow. I found it necessary to explain to one of my team members that they were not tears of sorrow, but it felt like every little bit of hardness of heart was being melted away and my heart was now like liquid love—God's love. That was another life-changing experience from which I have never recovered and trust that I never will.

I think that was what Paul was describing when he prayed for the Ephesian Christians that they, "*being rooted and grounded in love*," may understand its width, length, depth, and height and that they "*may be filled with all the fullness of God*" (Ephesians 3:17-19). We're only as filled with the Holy Spirit as we're filled with the love of God—to God first, then every member of His Body, and to the unconverted. Listen to the priority God places on this heart condition. "*Above **all things** have fervent love for one another*" (1 Peter 4:8).

Purification and Priorities

Another purpose for plowing is that the stones and weeds can be removed. The stones represent hindrances to spiritual progress, like wrong priorities. We need to have a continual check in that area of our lives and make the necessary adjustments.

1. Our responses to God's Word determine our goals.
2. Our goals determine our choices.
3. Our choices determine our character.
4. Our character determines our priorities.
5. Our priorities determine our destinies.

It is therefore crucial that we understand what our priorities are from God's Word. Genuine Christianity flows out of a love relationship with the Lord Jesus. And the daily infilling of the Holy Spirit, as we ask for it—"*Be filled with the Spirit*" (Ephesians 5:18)—equips us to do His will in the following four areas of major importance:

1. **Worship** and praise, and seeking His face and presence (see Psalm 34:1; 27:8; 105:4)
2. Time in God's **Word** getting to know Him and His ways (see Jeremiah 9:23-24; Psalm 25:4)
3. **Waiting** on God:

A. Making sure our hearts are clean from any undealt
   with sin (see Psalm 66:18).
B. For directions, guarding against all presumptions
   (see
   Psalm 19:13).
C. In intercession for others (see Isaiah 62:6-7).
4. **Witnessing** to others about the reality of Christ in our
   lives as a way of life (see Matthew 4:19; Acts 1:8).
   (Noting that each area starts with a "W" makes it easier
   to have a daily check.)

When there's a breakdown in any of these areas of our lives,
we know that we have need for serious "plowing" to remove the
boulders and stones that hinder the fulfillment of our destinies.
What better time than now to stop and have a reality check? What
things need to be removed in order to make time for God's priorities? Your destiny depends on it. And that's serious stuff.

The good is always the enemy of the best. It's also important
to know what our main ministry functions are so that we keep
within those parameters, and do not get sidetracked by the pressure from other people's requests and expectations or demands.

The weeds come as a result of neglect. We need to repent of
the sins of omission. "*To him who knows to do good and does not
do it, to him it is sin*" (James 4:17).

Remember, delayed obedience, partial obedience, and obedience with murmuring is all disobedience according to God's Word.
Disobedience represents a serious obstruction from weeds that
need to be plowed out. I will illustrate.

It was the teaching session on a Wednesday afternoon at a
spiritual leadership conference in the U.S.A., at which I was one
of three speakers. As I approached the hotel conference room, I
noticed that a man who had previously sat in the second row
from the front during all the other meetings, and who exuded an

enthusiastic, receptive spirit, was now standing at the outside edge of the room looking awkward.

When I inquired if I could help him, he explained that he was in severe pain down his right thigh and all the way down his right leg. He asked me to pray for him. I suggested that we go to the back of the room and sit down. When I asked the Lord what I was to do in this situation and quietly waited for His answer, not presuming anything, He responded by saying to me, "Tell him to ask Me what it is I am trying to teach him." I obeyed, and then the man thanked me, and fully cooperated, while I silently interceded that he would hear God's voice speaking into his spirit.

About ten minutes later I heard several deep muffled groans, and then the explanation. He said he had come under deep conviction of the sin of disobedience and that it was in every area of his life—disobedience to God in relation to his role as a husband, a father, a deacon in his church, and an employee of a business. In an anguished whisper, so as not to disturb others, he looked at me and said, "I'm riddled with it."

After thanking God for answering our sincere prayers, I encouraged the man to repent deeply before the Lord and to determine to follow through in obedience in every way in which God had instructed him as soon as he was able. He agreed. After a while I sought God again for His wisdom, and listened in silence. It was given, and in obedience, I simply laid my hand on the man's painful leg, asking God, in full faith in the authority of the name of the Lord Jesus Christ, to supernaturally touch him and release him from all pain.

About seven minutes later he reported, to his great relief, that the pain had started to subside in his thigh and then gradually went down his leg and that now he was pain-free. We thanked God for His mercy, while that dear deacon now understood in a new way what David meant when he said in Psalm 119:75, "*I know, O Lord, that Your judgments are right, and that in faithfulness You have afflicted me.*" Think of all the blessings that God could now heap upon that man when he obeyed God's orders.

In the first 14 verses of Deuteronomy 28, God promises to lavish His abundant blessings on every area of our lives if only we would obey Him. We do ourselves the greatest favor when we get the message and take God seriously. Don't you think it's kind of dumb to do anything else? Let's wise up, because the alternative is always grim. Read the last 54 verses of the same chapter—chapter 28. It's very sobering, to say the least.

The third purpose for plowing is so that new seeds can be planted. In the parable of the sower sowing his seed, Jesus clearly teaches us in Luke 8:11 that the seed is an illustration of the Word of God. We need to be seeking God expectantly, as a way of life for direct, fresh revelation of truth as we daily read His Word, so that we can walk in it. As we repent of everything that displeases Him, and walk in the light of God's truth, He encourages us from His Word that He will reveal more truth to us. It's one of His rewards. "*For with You is the fountain of truth. In Your light we see light*" (Psalm 36:9). We should never be content with only receiving secondhand revelation of truth. Jesus promised that the Holy Spirit would come and teach us all things. Believe Him. I suggest that you join me in praying like I do before I read my Bible, on a daily basis, "Dear God, reveal to me Your character and Your ways and open my eyes that I may behold wondrous things out of Your Word, as I submit myself in faith to the person of the Holy Spirit. Thank You that You will." By the way, disobedience is one of the greatest hindrances to revelation of truth. Why should God reveal more truth to us if we're not obedient to already revealed truth?

Another purpose for plowing is so that the rain can be received in deeper dimensions. How we need to stir ourselves up and commit to prioritizing prayer for genuine revival and spiritual awakening so that the rain of the Spirit can drench our lives, our churches, our cities, our nations. Zechariah 10:1 says, "*Ask the Lord for rain in the time of the latter rain. The Lord will make flashing clouds; He will give them showers of rain, grass in the field for everyone.*" In genuine revival God does more to extend His Kingdom in minutes, than what takes place in weeks, months, or years of God-ordained Christian activity. When that truth grips your heart, you don't need others to call you and prompt you to intercede for revival. You not only do so as a way of life, but you call others to do so.

Revival of the Church and spiritual awakening among the lost is the only answer to the desperate need of this hour and age. God promises us results to our desperate, persevering cries, from humble, clean, loving hearts. "*From the west, men will fear the name of the Lord and from the rising of the sun, they will revere His glory. For **He will come** like a pent up flood that the breath of the Lord drives along*" (Isaiah 59:19).

"*The Lord **will lay bare His holy arm** in the sight of all the nations and all the ends of the earth **will see** the salvation of our God*" (Isaiah 52:10).

The final purpose for plowing is that a more bountiful harvest can be reaped. As we cry out to God to give us a far greater spiritual ambition to be used by Him in this end-time harvest, He will answer us.

He's not looking for clever people, but clean people.

He's not looking for talented people, but available people.

He's not looking for people-pleasers, but for God-fearing people.

He's not looking for self-assured people, but on God-dependent-only people, people who have a passion for God and His glory.

He's not looking for people who can write a thesis on evangelism. He's looking for people with a burdened heart for the lost who will go out to where they are, love them, pray for them, weep for them, witness to them and be involved with their lives, and give their lives for the lost if necessary. *"Put in the sickle for the harvest is ripe...multitudes, multitudes in the valley of decision. For the day of the Lord is near..."* (Joel 3:13-14).

It's harvest time all over the world. That means that God has heard the cries of those of us who have been praying for the lost in every nation of the world, naming each nation separately, for numbers of decades. We've asked God to prepare the hearts of the unconverted in every nation so that when they hear the gospel they will immediately respond. We've asked God to reveal Himself in visions and dreams to the lost who have never heard the gospel. We've asked God to direct them to Christians who will explain to them the message of salvation and give them a Bible. It's happening. It's happening in every nation. It's harvest time.

We either are involved as a way of life in witnessing and winning people to Jesus and are therefore followers of Him, or we are disobedient and don't qualify to be a follower, according to Matthew 4:19. Jesus clearly said, *"Follow Me and I will make you fishers of men."*

Freedom Through Forgiveness

I don't know of a state of life that produces hardness of heart like the sin of resentment to those who have wronged us. We are such fragile beings. And we live in a fallen world where we seem to have the unique capacity of hurting each other whether out of our own humanness, or through our all too frequent misunderstanding of each other. The reality is that in this life we are going to get hurt to some degree or another. The greater the hurt, the deeper the pain. The deeper the pain, the more tempted we are to yield to the force of resentment to the perpetrator of the pain. That's the human reaction.

Without the stronger healing force of forgiveness we become subject to the utter bondage, the slavery, the destructive force of unforgiveness. *"A sound heart is life to the body but envy is rottenness to the bones"* (Psalm 14:30).

It is important for us to understand that the purposes of the fire of God's love in our lives are often parallel to the purposes of natural fire. Natural fire melts hard substances. The Lord yearns for us to believe that He alone knows the extent of our hurt and pain because there is nothing hidden from His sight. More than that, because the Lord Jesus has paid the ultimate price of suffering when He became our substitute and sin-bearer on the cross, we read in Psalm 147:5 that *"His understanding is infinite* [or unsearchable].*"* Think about that. That's why He can promise in Psalm 147:3 that, *"He heals the broken hearted and binds up their wounds."* So, He knows everything, understands everything, and can fix everything. We can't beat that for a deal!

With that in mind, let us come to Him with our wounded spirits and cry out like David did in Psalm 22:19, *"But You, O Lord, do not be far from me, O my strength; hasten to help me."* In this case, "Hasten to help us, by enabling us to forgive every person who has hurt us."

I recently read in a book written by a Christian doctor, where he quoted a veteran doctor who stated that he had never seen a more destructive force on the human body than the root of bitterness. The writer went on to say that he had personally witnessed this phenomenon in his own practice, having completed over 100,000 patient visits. Impressive stats!

It is perfectly possible, in our ignorance, to have resentment toward God. But because the Bible tells us in Deuteronomy 32:4

that "*He is the Rock, His work is perfect; for all His ways are justice, a God of truth and without injustice; righteous and upright is He*," it is therefore impossible to charge Him with blame. Therefore He doesn't qualify for our forgiveness. We can only forgive people who have wronged us. However, we must not presume that because we're feeling hurt, that the person connected with the pain was necessarily guilty of doing wrong.

Let's look at some reasons for feeling hurt, where we could be tempted to wrongly judge people:

1. We were not consulted before a decision was made. Perhaps we were not meant to be involved in that responsibility.
2. We were not told about something for which we should have been informed. Maybe the breakdown of communication was with someone else who had been delegated to do so and had failed.
3. We were not given the attention we requested from an individual, or insufficient attention for our liking. It could be, that for a number of reasons our receiving attention was not a legitimate priority for that individual at that time, or their amount of availability was equally limited.
4. We were not given the recognition for our labors that we thought we deserved. Perhaps God overruled the recognition by withholding it in order to test the motivation of our hearts. Jesus said, "*I do not receive praise from men*," simply because He gave all the glory to the Father.
5. We were corrected by someone where we considered the judgment to be unfair. Maybe we were immediately defensive and didn't have the humility to ask God to show us if there was even a small percentage of truth in their overall judgment.
6. We were seemingly ignored by someone when we were in the presence of others. It's absolutely possible that the

person either didn't see us, or never heard us, or for any number of reasons wasn't able to speak or respond to us. For example, it could be because of the pressures of responsibilities on the person, or their physical condition, or because they were under great stress, to name a few.

7. We were not included in a group situation where we thought we should have been. It could be that there was an unexplainable oversight, or perhaps the group felt it would be wiser and more beneficial for all concerned, including ourselves, if we were not included.

We need to honestly ask the Holy Spirit to show us where our ego and pride may have been the cause of our pain when we're feeling offended. When we really come to the place of death to that monster called self and want it to be crucified, we enter into real freedom. You can't offend a dead man.

On the other hand, there are times when others have totally distorted our characters through what they've said about us, or have perpetuated lies about us. That's another story, and God understands the pain that comes from those experiences. If we will forgive them, He will heal us and vindicate us in His way and time (see Isaiah 54:17).

We also need to be far more sensitive in all our communications with each other. Here's a check list:

1. Is the communication really necessary?
2. Is it our responsibility to communicate, or another's?
3. Are we communicating in the right timing?
4. Have we the right method of communicating?
5. Are we in the right attitude of heart? Have we checked our motives?
6. Are we prepared to speak only 100 percent truth in humility, gentleness, love, and graciousness?

In Luke 12:48 (RSV), Jesus said, *"Everyone to whom much is given, of him will much be required; and of him to whom men commit much they will **demand** the more."*

We need to be especially sensitive to everything related to our communications with spiritual leaders. They are subject to a great deal of unnecessary stress by virtue of their high profile, from people who, often in ignorance, create that stress. Let's heed this admonition so that it can be avoided.

If we have wrongly judged others, God requires repentance of that sin, because Matthew 7:1-2 says, *"Judge not that you be not judged, for with what judgment you judge you will be judged."* Only repentance will release us from God's judgment that is already on us. If we have shared our wrong judgment with others, we will also need to make restitution by telling them.

How much disunity in the Body of Christ would be avoided if only we would live by the Word of God. In Matthew 5:23-24, Jesus said that if we know another person has something against us, we're to go to that person and seek reconciliation. Also, if someone has sinned against us, we're to go to him or her *alone* and express our forgiveness and do everything we know to be reconciled (see Matthew 18:15).

I know of two spiritual leaders who drifted apart from the close fellowship they had previously enjoyed, only to discover that there was a major misunderstanding between them that went back over decades. Neither of them had operated on the Scriptures I have quoted above. How sad.

How grateful I've been on a couple of occasions when dear friends have asked me if there was anything I knew that would have caused our friendship not to be what it was; only for me to warmly and strongly assure them that nothing had changed from my perspective, and then to be able to give them an explanation for their inquiry. This resulted in closer unity, and potential misunderstandings were avoided.

Unity in Christ's Body of believers is the most powerful influence for unbelievers to be convinced that the Lord Jesus is the Son of God and that God loves His disciples as He loved His Son. What an incredible impact! That's why forgiveness is so essential for world evangelization (see John 17:23).

How to Forgive

God's Word says, "*Looking carefully lest anyone fall short of the grace of God; lest any root of bitterness springing up cause trouble, and by this many become defiled*" (Hebrews 12:15). Obviously, from this Scripture there is enough of God's grace available to enable any one of us to forgive an offense.

The following scriptural principles, when put into practice, will release anyone into the full freedom of forgiveness. They have been tried and proven true.

1. Realize that forgiveness is an act of the will. We have to want to forgive. Some people simply don't want to. They prefer to harbor their resentment and continue in their bondage.
2. Understand that resentment is destructive to the mind, body, soul, and spirit. "*A tranquil mind gives life to the flesh, but envy makes the bones rot*" (Proverbs 14:30 RSV).
3. Realize that we will not be forgiven by God unless we forgive those who have hurt us. "*And when you stand praying if you hold anything against anyone, forgive him, so that your Father in heaven may forgive your sins*" (Mark 11:25). Wow! That's heavy! Is there anyone who doesn't need God's ongoing forgiveness?

4. Think of all that God has forgiven us. "*Be kind and compassionate to one another, forgiving each other, just as in Christ, God forgave you*" (Ephesians 4:32). "*As the Lord has forgiven you, so you must also forgive*" (Colossians 3:13b). God forgives us instantly, joyfully, and wholly.

5. Thank the Lord for any or all of the blessings He has brought to us through the people who have hurt us. Write them down. Thankfulness and resentment have a hard time remaining together.

6. Think of the needs—mental, physical, emotional, and spiritual—of the individuals at the time of their hurting us. Their needs then—and now—are probably greater than ours.

7. We ask God to give us His supernatural ability to love and forgive those people. Acknowledge that this is the work of the Holy Spirit and receive it by faith. "*God has poured out His love into our hearts by the Holy Spirit, whom He has given us*" (Romans 5:5b). "*And without faith, it is impossible to please God*" (Hebrews 11:6a). "*Faith* [expresses] *itself through love*" (Galatians 5:6). And God has promised in First Corinthians 13:8a that "*love never fails.*"

8. We ask God for opportunities to express His love to these people both in word and in deed. "*Dear children, let us not love with words or tongue but with actions and in truth*" (1 John 3:17-18). Benevolent acts and expressed love make it terribly hard for resentment to exist. They suffocate it.

9. Become a regular intercessor for them. Pray only for God to bless them, encourage them, comfort them, strengthen them, and meet their deepest needs. "*But I tell you: love your enemies and pray for those who persecute you*" (Matthew 5:44).

As we persist in these spiritual exercises we find we are being conformed into the image of the Lord Jesus, and after all, that's our goal; so that makes us express gratitude to God for allowing the painful circumstances in the first place. And we've again proved that His matchless grace has brought us through. What a God!

Who to Forgive

The deeper we love people the more we will suffer when hurt by them, particularly where injustice is involved. Therefore, the ones we need to forgive the most are often those closest to us in relationships.

Let us check through the list for any hidden resentments: wives, husbands, fathers, mothers, friends, schoolteachers, spiritual leaders, people we've been teamed with in ministries, people with whom we work, people over us in authority, people under our authority, politicians and government officials from our own nation or other nations, governments that have hurt those who are close to us, and any other categories you know of. Unfortunately there are times when, in their human frailty, spiritual leaders misjudge us. The greatest saints who have ever lived have all had clay feet, so don't expect perfection.

Often leaders, because of the weight of their many responsibilities, react too quickly and make wrong judgments of others. We need to learn from Hannah in First Samuel 1, how to pass this kind of difficult test if we are the one who is hurt. Eli the priest totally misjudged the godly woman Hannah, in the temple, when she was fasting and quietly pouring out her anguished heart to the Lord in prayer. Eli accused her of drunkenness and rebuked her. How painful; how unjust. The very person who should have been the one to minister comfort, understanding, and encouragement to her in her hour of need, was an instrument of great pain.

Hannah's name means "grace" and this beautiful quality of the Holy Spirit was evident when she respectfully addressed him and gently explained what she was doing. Immediately, Eli prophesied a blessing from God over her, telling her that her prayers were heard and fulfillment was on the way. Obviously Hannah knew that she needed to instantly forgive her spiritual leader to have favor with God. By doing so, God was able to release the word of the Lord through Eli to bless her. If we hold resentment in our hearts to spiritual leaders who have hurt us, we will not be able to receive the many blessings through them that God has planned to give us. Thank God that His mercy is always extended to a truly repentant heart.

Now let's learn from a spiritual leader who failed to forgive a person under his authority. As we carefully read through the events of the story in Second Samuel 13, of Absalom murdering his brother Amnon, we find in verses 37-39 that Absalom then fled and went to another city for three years. David mourned for him every day and longed to go to him. But David, as his leader, never confronted Absalom, or disciplined him, or sought for reconciliation with him.

Joab, David's military leader, and a wise woman from the city of Tekoa were both used by God to get the message through to David that he needed to invite Absalom back home. If David had forgiven his son, he wouldn't have needed all that input. Then, when Absalom did return home it was on the condition that Absalom was not to see David's face. Second Samuel 14:24 says, *"And the king said, 'Let him return to his own house, but do not let him see my face.'"* In verse 28 we're told that Absalom was in Jerusalem for two full years but did not see the king's face.

After that, Absalom tried on two occasions to get Joab to go to King David on his behalf, to try to get permission for Absalom to see his father. Finally that worked out and we read these words, "*So Joab went to the king and told him. And when he had called for Absalom, he came to the king and bowed himself on his face to the ground before the king. Then the king kissed Absalom*" (verse 33). Superficially it looks as if everything is okay. But it's not. There's not a word written about any communication, reconciliation, or fellowship. And without fellowship of some kind there's no restoration of relationship. Conversely, forgiveness will always lead to fellowship.

In chapter 15 of Second Samuel, in verse 1 it reads, "*After this it happened....*" It was the start of Absalom's schemes of winning the hearts of the people to himself, which finally ended in open revolt and betrayal. I believe that David's lack of forgiveness became a cause of temptation to Absalom to betray his father. In Matthew 18:7 Jesus gives us a solemn warning about being a cause of temptation to others: "*Woe to the world because of offenses. For offenses must come, but woe to the man by whom the offense comes.*" And in James 3:1 God states that those who teach God's Word are more accountable to God than the hearers of His Word.

David's lack of forgiveness brought not only God's disapproval on his life, but further great suffering to the people he led. And that's another long story, which is told in the ensuing chapters of Second Samuel.

To conclude this section on the fire of God's love to purify us, I invite you to pray with me the following powerful, penetrating poem by Shirley Crow.

Change Me[5]
Dear Lord, change not Thy will in my life,
Or trial and sorrow to be.
Renew my faith, and make me strong,

Change not Thy will, Lord, change me.

Though tear drops fall when trouble comes,

Like a storm on a rolling sea,

Let Thy beacon guide my ship to port,

Change not the storm, Lord, change me.

When Thy holy Word I don't understand,

And Thy glory I cannot see,

Teach my eyes, give me sight and wisdom,

Change not Thy Word, Lord, change me.

If the fruit Thou hast given me to eat

Taste bitter and sour, I plead,

Let not my will but Thine be done,

Change not the fruit, Lord, change me.

If sometimes I murmur and grumble, dear Lord,

About the cross I carry for Thee,

Keep it firm on my shoulders, but hold my hand,

Change not the cross, change me.

If You change Your ways to please me, dear Lord,

I would soon grow cold and turn from Thee

That You would hear my prayers, dear Lord,

Change not Thy ways Lord, change me.

There's a valley that I must cross,

Some day Thy face to see,

Lest I forget what powers are Thine,

Change not the valley, Lord, change me.

~ Shirley Crow

PREPARATION FOR REVIVAL FIRE

R evival is where the fire of God so invades the affairs of men that they see and experience the amplified version of Him, in technicolor and quadraphonic stereo. *"Out of Zion, the perfection of beauty, God will shine forth. Our God shall come and shall not keep silent; a fire shall devour before Him and it shall be very tempestuous all around Him"* (Psalm 50:2-3).

Revival is the awesome, sustained, manifest presence of God that changes the moral and spiritual life of a community and culture. Revival is the sovereign outpouring of the Holy Spirit in God's way and time, first of all upon God's people. The revelation of God's holiness is strongly accentuated and, as a result, God's viewpoint on sin is revealed. Everyone, young and old, has the opportunity to deeply repent or harden their hearts against the convicting power of the Holy Spirit.

During an outpouring of the Holy Spirit among the Zulus in South Africa, about 30 years ago, many people were openly repenting of sin, and then experiencing great joy in the Lord. But not all. On one occasion, out of a clear blue sky with no sign of rain, suddenly forked lightning struck the church building on one side only, resulting in a large crack on the inside wall in one specific place.

Immediately, a Christian man cried out. "It's me. It's because of me!" The crack occurred right beside where he was sitting. In deep repentance he explained that he had been immoral and had resisted the Holy Spirit's conviction and had not been willing to acknowledge his sin until now.

A spiritual leader friend of mine visited that place not long after and told me that the pastors purposely left the large crack in the unmended wall. My friend saw it. It was a constant reminder to all that when we pray for revival we can expect that everything about God's manifest presence will be accelerated and it will certainly not be church as usual.

It was also a reminder of the truth of Luke 8:17: "*For nothing is secret that will not be revealed nor anything hidden that will not be known and come to light*" (if we don't first bring it to the light in repentance, and make restitution where needed).

Revival is God greatly stirring, shaking, and changing His people from apathy, selfishness, and self-promotion to a desperate, praying, humble, honest, and contrite people with a passion for God Himself and His glory and a deep burden for the lost.

Revival is the fullest expression of the life of the Lord Jesus in every believer. A great spiritual awakening among lost souls also takes place, and multitudes of hardened sinners deeply repent of their sin and commit their lives to the Lord Jesus Christ. Revival is not evangelism but revival inevitably includes a great increase in effective evangelism. A change of the culture toward righteousness takes place. This was vividly demonstrated in the revival in the Hebrides Islands, off the coast of Scotland.

The following report is an adaptation of quotations from the biography of Duncan Campbell.

The presence of God was a universal, inescapable fact: at home, in the church and by the roadside. The very air seemed to be tingling with divine vitality. One night a man came to a manse in great concern. The minister brought him into the study and asked, "What touched you? I haven't seen you at any of the services." "No," he replied. "I haven't been to church, but this revival is in the air. I can't get away from the Spirit."[6]

In another part the biographer writes:

In the fields or at the weaving looms, men were overcome and prostrated on the ground before God. One said: "The grass beneath my feet and the rocks around me seem to cry: 'Flee to Christ for refuge!'" The agony of conviction was terrible to behold, but Duncan [Campbell] rejoiced knowing that out of the deep travail would be born a rich, virile Christian experience, unlike the cheap, easy-going 'believe-ism' that produces no radical moral change.[7]

In the Hebrides revival, thousands of young people were converted and they would go to cottage meetings at 10 P.M. *after* the meetings in the churches. The oldest people on the Hebrides Islands have been through three revivals (that we know of). Every morning and every evening in every home they conduct family worship. The Christians have a short prayer, read a Psalm, sing a Psalm, and read one chapter of the Bible. The non-Christians read a Psalm, one chapter of the Bible, and have a prayer. Every respectable young couple just before marriage receives a family Bible and is expected to conduct family prayers every morning. Everyone observes the Sabbath very carefully. No manual work is done because it is the Lord's Day. In day-school the children are taught to memorize portions of the Word of God, and every month a minister comes to hear them recite it.[8] Revivals have affected their culture.

In the history of genuine revivals, God shows up first in a display of His awesome holiness and pristine purity—because that's the part of His character to which we most need to be exposed. We'll never remotely understand God's incredible humility and unfathomable love until we've understood His awesome holiness. That's the part of God's character that the seraphim and the living creatures sing about all the time before the throne of God in Heaven.

When we experience the fire of God's power on our bodies, we may lie down on the floor on our backs, face up. Sometimes there is great change in one or more areas of our lives. But sometimes there is relatively little change to our spiritual lives. The children of Israel saw the wonder of God's breathtaking power in epic proportions, but it never changed their lives.

Whereas, when we are exposed to more than an average degree of God's holiness, we usually lie prostrate on the floor, face down. It was so with Daniel the prophet and the apostle John and the prophet Ezekiel who had those sort of encounters with Almightyness. And those encounters had by far the most life-changing results.

In Daniel 10 we read that after 21 days of fasting and praying, Daniel had a revelation of the Lord Jesus. *"His body was like beryl, his face like the appearance of lightning, his eyes like torches of fire, his arms and his feet like burnished bronze in color and the sound of his words like the voice of a multitude."* This left Daniel totally depleted of all strength, lying down with his face to the ground.

In Ezekiel 2:22 we read that the hand of the Lord was on Ezekiel and he was told to go out into the plain because God wanted to talk to him. Verse 23 says that when Ezekiel obeyed, *"The glory of the Lord stood there...and **I fell on my face.**"*

In Revelation 1:9-16 we read that John was on the island of Patmos in exile when he heard God speaking in a loud voice instructing him to write in a book what he was about to be shown. When he turned to look at who had spoken, he saw the truly awesome sight of the Lord in His magnificent splendor, His blazing glory, and pristine purity. *"His head and hair were white like wool, as white as snow, and His eyes like a flame of fire. His feet were like fine brass, as if refined in a furnace. His voice as the sound of many waters! He had in His right hand seven stars. Out of His mouth went a sharp two-edged sword. His countenance was like the sun shining in its strength."*

John's reaction to this incomprehensible exposure of mystery and majesty was simply to pass right out. His human, finite frailty gave way under the weight of the infinite grandeur of Deity. The Bible simply says, *"John fell at His feet as dead."*

To me, that's the only appropriate response! Thank God, He's good at resurrections and delights at saying His favorite line, *"Don't be afraid, I've got everything under control. I've been around a long while."* That's my paraphrase of verse 17.

In genuine revival, God does more to extend His Kingdom in seconds or minutes than in days, weeks, months, or years of God-inspired and energized Christian activity. The course of history toward righteousness can be changed in a nation quicker than any other way through genuine revival. The following account vividly illustrates this significant point. Oswald Smith describes a revival in Hawaii:

> In the year 1835 Titus Coan landed on the shore belt of Hawaii. On his first tour multitudes flocked to hear him. They thronged him so that he had scarcely time to eat. Once, he preached three times before he had a chance to take breakfast. He knew that God was deeply at work. In 1837 the slumbering fires broke out. Nearly the whole

population became an audience. He was ministering to 15,000 people. Unable to reach them, they came to him, and settled down to a two years' camp meeting. There was not an hour, day or night, when an audience from 2,000 to 6,000 would not rally to the signal of a bell. There was trembling, weeping, sobbing and loud crying out for mercy, sometimes too loud for the preacher to be heard; and in hundreds of cases his hearers fell down under the power of God. Some would cry out, "The two-edged sword is cutting me to pieces." The wicked scoffer who came to make sport dropped like a dog, and cried, "God has struck me!" Once while preaching in the open field to 2,000 people, a man cried out, "What must I do to be saved?" and prayed the publican's prayer, and the entire congregation took up the cry for mercy. For half an hour Mr. Coan could get no chance to preach, but had to stand still and see God work. Quarrels were made up, drunkards reclaimed, adulterers converted, and murderers revealed and pardoned. Thieves returned stolen property. And sins of a lifetime were renounced. In one year 5,244 joined the Church. There were 1,705 baptized on one Sunday. And 2,400 sat down at the Lord's table, once sinners of the blackest type, now saints of God. And when Mr. Coan left, he had himself baptized 11,960 persons.[9]

When people advertise that they are going to hold a revival, they obviously have a totally different understanding of the biblical concept of revival, and they could never have seriously studied the history of genuine spiritual awakenings.

Only God can start a revival. Man can stop one through resisting, quenching, and grieving the Holy Spirit. Only God knows when He's going to respond to the united cries of His people and unleash the Holy Spirit as described in Psalm 45:3-4: "*Gird Your sword upon Your thigh, O Mighty One, with Your glory* *and Your majesty. And in Your majesty ride prosperously because of truth, humility and righteousness; and Your right hand shall teach You **awesome things**.*"

Awesome things! That's what takes place in true revival. Unfortunately that word is bandied around and frequently used to describe the relatively puny. We're left with no adjective to describe what is only rightly attributable to Deity. ***Only God and His work and His ways are awesome***.

The unpredictable and the unusual become normal in real revival. God has warned us from His Word that He can work this way. "*I have made you hear new things from this time, even hidden things, and you did not know them. They are created now and not from the beginning. And before this day you have not heard them*" (Isaiah 48:6-7).

Listen to another Scripture where God describes His transcendent, limitless greatness, His other-than-normal-ness, His altogether other-worldly-ness: "*For the Lord will rise up as at Mount Perazim* [when God broke through David's enemies and defeated them, and David called God, 'The Master of Breakthrough'], *He will be angry as in the valley of Gibeon* [after Joshua and his army had marched all night, they descended suddenly upon their enemies, and the Bible says], *God routed them...killed them...and struck them down...and then cast down large hailstones from Heaven on them.... And they died.*" With that backdrop of a display of God's awesome power, without even having to flex His muscles, God goes on to give us a sneak preview into what things might look like when He really shows up in revival: "***That He may do His work, His awesome work, and bring to pass His act, His unusual act***" (Isaiah 28:21).

This Scripture is vividly illustrated in a quote from David Brainerd, a mighty intercessor who describes the revival among the American Indians:

The power of God seemed to descend upon the assembly like a mighty, rushing wind, and with an astonishing energy bore down all before it. I stood amazed at the influence, which seized the audience almost universally; and could compare it to nothing more than the irresistible force of a mighty torrent.... Almost all persons of all ages including children were bowed down and in deep distress over the state of their souls, oblivious to those around them. They were universally praying and crying out for mercy in every part of the building, and many out of doors.[10]

In Arthur Wallis's book *The Rain From Heaven*, he writes, "In revival man becomes oblivious of everyone else but himself in the agonizing grip of a holy God."[11]

Another biblical description of an unpredictable, sustained outpouring of the Holy Spirit is found in Isaiah 64:3, as the prophet Isaiah pours out his impassioned cry to God:

"O that You would rend the heavens. That You would come down! That the mountains might shake at Your presence. As fire burns brushwood, as fire causes water to boil. To make Your name known to Your adversaries. That the nations may tremble at Your presence. **When You did awesome things for which we did not look**, *You came down, the mountains shook at Your presence."*

"Oh God, my heart cries out again, "Restore us to Yourself that we may return..." (Lamentations 5:21).

"Will You not revive us again, that Your people may rejoice in You?" (Psalm 85:6)

God, come and do something in us that only You can do that will powerfully motivate us to deeply repent of all idolatry—everything that keeps us from making You our supreme longing, first love, and greatest purpose for living. We humble ourselves before You, Father, and identify with David and say, "My soul cleaves to the dust; revive me according to Your

Word" (Ps. 119:25 NASB). (To me, that means we're very prone to prioritize earthly pursuits.) Lord, speak to us again from Your Word and inspire and ignite our souls with the flame of Your Spirit to more fervently pursue eternal things. In Jesus' mighty and all powerful name. Amen.

Church history has recorded times when the most devout spiritual leaders who prayed for revival were the first to initially oppose it, largely because they had little idea of what characterizes revival. In light of that we need to ask ourselves some pertinent questions.

Cooperation or Control?

Do we understand that revival is on God's terms and do we really want it?

Have we studied revivals in the Word of God and read extensively on subsequent revivals?

Would we recognize the flood-tide of God's presence, or would we resist it?

Would we cooperate with God or try to control the unusual or the unpredictable?

"From the west, men will fear the name of the Lord, and from the rising of the sun they will revere His glory. For He will come like a pent-up flood that the breath of the Lord drives along" (Isaiah 59:19 NIV).

The following account is adapted from Edwin Orr's book, *The Fervent Prayer.*

In Worcester, in the Cape Province of South Africa, an outbreak of the Holy Spirit came one Sunday evening when 60 young people were gathered in a hall and were being led in intercession by J.C. deVries, an assistant to Rev. Andrew Murray. Several had requested the singing of a hymn, and some had offered a prayer, when a Fingo girl who was employed by a farmer, asked if she could do the same. Permission was hesitatingly granted. (The Fingos were the lowest strata of society.)

While she was praying, a noise like rolling thunder was heard coming closer and closer until it enveloped the hall, shaking the whole place. Everyone spontaneously burst into audible prayer, aware that an unusual outpouring of the Holy Spirit appeared to be taking place. We need to understand that in a Dutch Reformed Church in South Africa around 1858, what has just been described would be very abnormal, to say the least.

Andrew Murray had just finished preaching the regular Sunday evening message in his church when he was notified of the unusual outbreak among the young people. To his amazement, when he went, he saw his assistant pastor kneeling at a table without any sign of trying to control the unusual manifestation as the simultaneous audible prayers continued.

Andrew Murray walked among the people, calling out for them to be quiet, but no one took the slightest notice. Finally he shouted, "I am your minister, sent from God. Silence!" Again no one responded and the prayers continued. Each person seemed more concerned with calling on God for forgiveness of an intolerable weight of sin, while deVries kept kneeling at the table in holy awe at the Divine visitation.

After Andrew Murray tried unsuccessfully to get the people to sing a hymn, he left the hall in bewilderment, exclaiming, "God is a God of order and here everything is in confusion." DeVries continued in silent prayer, overwhelmed at God's awesome presence.

Nightly meetings were held in the little hall, usually beginning in a period of profound silence. Then the place became shaken as before as everyone engaged in simultaneous, fervent petition at the throne of grace. The meetings often continued until three in the morning, when the people returned home, singing praises to God through the sleeping town.

Because of crowded attendances, the meetings were moved to a larger building, which soon filled up. On the first night, Andrew Murray read some Scriptures, gave a message from the Bible, and then prayed. Again the mysterious roll of approaching thunder was heard, coming nearer and nearer until it enveloped the building. The spontaneous, audible prayer broke out again with Andrew Murray walking up and down the aisles trying to quiet the people.

Finally, a stranger who had recently come from America where he had seen the outpouring of God's Spirit in revival, quietly approached Andrew Murray and whispered to him, "I understand that you are the minister of this congregation. Be careful what you do, for it is the Spirit of God at work here."

Later, when Andrew Murray got alone with God and asked Him to show him what was going on, the Holy Spirit assured him that what was happening was of Himself. This dear minister repented of trying to control the people and acknowledged in brokenness before God and man that he had been hindering the deep work of the Holy Spirit among them.

Subsequently, he was greatly used of God in the sustained outpouring of the Holy Spirit that spread through other parts of South Africa at that time. Through Andrew Murray's deep teaching and writing ministries, untold multitudes worldwide have been influenced to become more like Jesus. I am one of them.

Let us learn from this great man of God's life and testimony. He specialized in pursuing humility like few I have ever heard of. His book on this subject is a classic.

Pursuing Humility

I believe that one of our greatest universal needs is to obey the injunction given to us from Zephaniah 2:3: *"Seek the Lord, all you meek of the earth, who have upheld His justice. Seek righteousness, **seek humility**."*

God promises personal revival to every life who pursues humility. *"For thus says the High and lofty One who inhabits eternity, whose name is Holy. I dwell in the high and holy place with him who has a contrite and humble spirit. To revive the spirit of the humble and to revive the hearts of the contrite ones"* (Isaiah 57:15). Now that's great news!

Humility was certainly a marked characteristic of the outpouring of the Holy Spirit at Azusa Street, Los Angeles, in 1906. The following is a quotation from the book, *What Happened at Azusa Street.*

> *The services ran almost continuously. Seeking souls* could be found under the power almost any hour, night and day. The place was never closed nor empty. The people came to meet God. He was always there. Hence a continuous meeting. The meetings did not depend on a human leader. God's presence became more and more wonderful. In that old building, with its low rafters and bare floors, God took strong men and women to pieces, and put them together again, for His glory. It was a tremendous overhauling process. Pride and self-assertion, self-importance and self-esteem could not survive there. The religious ego preached its own funeral sermon quickly.

No subjects or sermons were announced ahead of time, and no special speakers for such an hour. No one knew what might be coming, what God would do. ...The rich and the educated were the same as the poor and the ignorant, and found a much harder death to die. ...When we first reached the meeting, we avoided as much as possible of human contact and greeting. We wanted to meet God first. We got our head under some bench in the corner in prayer, and met men only in the Spirit, knowing them "after the flesh no more."[12]

*The depth of longing in my heart for that kind of visitation of the Spirit again is impossible to convey in words. I can only keep crying out to God and say, "The need for You to unleash the Holy Spirit upon us, Your people, **today** to produce that kind of humility is far greater now than then. From Your Word we know that satan cannot understand genuine Christlike humility because he's so consumed by pride. So, do whatever it takes in us, Your people, to produce this all-powerful weapon of humility that will outwit him and nullify his tactics. In Jesus' name, I believe. Amen."*

One of the most significant and thrilling accounts of humility in a spiritual leader comes out of the Hebrides revival. It concerns Duncan Campbell and a young teenager named Donald McPhail who was converted in the revival at the age of 15 and who was mightily used of God.

The most outstanding example of God's anointing upon him was in Bernera, a small island off the coast of Lewis. Duncan was assisting at a communion season; the atmosphere was heavy and preaching difficult, so he sent to Barvas for some of the men to come and assist in prayer. They prayed, but the spiritual bondage persisted, so much so that half way through his address, Duncan stopped preaching. Just then he noticed this boy, visibly moved under a deep burden for souls. He thought: "That boy is in touch with God and living nearer to the Savior than I am." So leaning over the pulpit he said, "Donald, will you lead us in prayer?"

The lad rose to his feet and in his prayer made reference to the fourth chapter of Revelation, which he had been reading that morning: "O God, I seem to be gazing through the open door. I see the Lamb in the midst of the Throne, with the keys of death and hell at His girdle." He began to sob; then lifting his eyes toward heaven, cried; "O God, there is power there, let it loose!" With the force of a hurricane the Spirit of God swept into the building and the floodgates of Heaven opened. The church resembled a battlefield. On one side many were prostrated over the seats weeping and sighing; on the other side some were affected by throwing their arms in the air in a rigid posture, God had come.[13]

Again, I wonder how many spiritual leaders today would have the genuine Christlike humility of recognizing that a recently converted teenager needed to be released to minister in some way for God's floodgates to be opened? There is a hunger for God, combined with a passion for Jesus, and a burden for lost souls upon this generation of young people that is totally God-breathed and God-birthed and is destined to make history in these times.

Those of us who are outside of that generation in age had better recognize this and allow the Holy Spirit to do the deep work of humility needed in our hearts to cooperate with God's end-time purposes through this young, radical-for-God army. If we don't, we'll find ourselves bypassed.

If we do, we'll find ourselves privileged to be trusted by God with some of the most awesome ministry assignments of our lives. I, for one, am constantly being refreshed, invigorated, and blessed out of my socks as I do myself a favor by having some of them as my close friends.

We must also never underestimate the work of the Holy Spirit coming upon and working through children. In 1805 at Aberystwyth in Wales, there was a powerful awakening which began in a Sunday school established by two young laymen. One of them was leaving Aberystwyth and was engaged in fervent prayer for his young charges, when the Holy Spirit fell upon him and the children so powerfully that "the whole gathering became lost in tears and demonstrations."

In the spiritual awakening that followed it was reported that hundreds of children from eight years old and upward could be seen in the congregations of at least 20,000 people. While bathed in tears, these children were listening to the powerful preaching of the Word of God with all the attentiveness of the most devout Christians.[14]

In 1859, in Ulster, Ireland, during a school class in the town of Coloraine, a boy came under such deep conviction of sin, that a kind teacher sent him home with another boy who was a Christian. On the way home, the Christian boy led the troubled boy to Christ. Immediately they returned to the class, and the new convert said to the teacher, "I am so happy. I have the Lord Jesus in my heart."

This innocent testimony had a remarkable effect, as boy after boy rose and left the class. The teacher found them kneeling and praying around the courtyard, each apart. The sound of their cries of conviction reached the girls' schoolroom, which resulted in the whole school being on their knees in deep conviction.

Soon, parents and friends were alerted and arrived. Along with the teachers, everyone came under the influence of this outpouring of the Holy Spirit as they sought for peace with God. This went on until 11 P.M., with the help of ministers who were asked to come. These happenings stirred the whole district.[15]

The Big Picture

In closing this section on revival fires, I believe we need to see the big picture of divine purposes, in order to have the vision we need to give this subject the priority God intends.

- **Nothing defeats satan's purposes and plans to keep God's people in lethargy and complacency like revival.**
- **Nothing defeats satan's purposes and plans in blinding the eyes of the unconverted to the truth of the gospel like a great spiritual awakening.**
- **Satanic forces aren't so much concerned with how much Christian activity we're involved in, as long as we don't get desperate for an invasion of the Holy Spirit, where God takes over.**
- **There is no better preparation for the inevitable, increased persecution coming to the Church universal than revival.**

The Bible warns us that "*all who desire to live godly in Christ Jesus will suffer persecution. But evil men and imposters will grow worse and worse, deceiving and being deceived*" (2 Timothy 3:12-13).

The early Church is a perfect example. It was launched in revival, and not only survived intense persecution but thrived and multiplied. Its opponents declared in Acts 17:6 that "*They turned the world upside down.*"

The Church in revival in the Congo in Africa in the early 1950s before the Cimbas wrought havoc is another example. It is recorded in the book entitled *This Is That*, published by Worldwide Evangelization Crusade.

The Church in revival in Cambodia in the 1970s, before severe persecution hit, is another. Todd Burke was a missionary in

Cambodia at the time and has written a gripping account in his wonderful book, *Anointed for Burial.*

- **There is no better means of preparing the Church to become the Bride of Christ than genuine revival.**

"Christ also loved the Church and gave Himself for her that He might sanctify her and cleanse her with the washing of water by the Word, that He might present her to Himself, a glorious Church, not having spot or wrinkle or any such thing, but that she should be holy and without blemish" (Ephesians 5:25-27). Nothing purges and purifies the Church like God's revival fires because conviction of sin is a major feature of revival.

During the revival in the U.S.A. in the early 1800s during Charles Finney's time, we read from Oswald J. Smith's book, *The Revival We Need*, that "When he arrived at a place he found the people already crying out for mercy. Sometimes the conviction of sin was so great and caused such fearful wails of anguish that he had to stop preaching until it subsided. Ministers and church members were converted."[16]

- **Nothing will speed up the coming again of the Lord Jesus, like revival.**

"But the day of the Lord will come like a thief. The heavens will disappear with a roar; the elements will be destroyed by fire and the earth and everything in it will be laid bare. Since everything will be destroyed in this way, what kind of people ought you to be? You ought to live holy and godly lives as you look forward to the day of God and **speed its coming**" (2 Peter 3:10-12 NIV).

Verse 14 of that same chapter says *"Since you are looking to this, make every effort to be found spotless, blameless and at peace with Him."*

- **Nothing will better prepare the Church for the Judgment Seat of Christ than revival.**

"Our God comes and will not be silent; a fire devours before Him, and around Him a tempest rages. He summons the earth that He may judge His people" (Psalm 50:3-4 NIV); *"...for we shall all stand before the judgment seat of Christ.... Each of us shall give account of himself to God"* (Romans 14:10-12).

- **The course of history in turning a nation to righteousness is changed quicker than any other way through a revived Church and a great spiritual awakening among the unconverted.**

What God did in and through the Welsh revival is a classic example of this truth. In Dr. J. Edwin Orr's book on *Evangelical Awakenings 1900, Worldwide*, we read:

> The Welsh revival was the farthest reaching of the movements of the general Awakening for it affected the whole of the evangelical cause in India, Korea and China; renewed revival in Japan and South Africa and sent the wave of Awakening over Africa, Latin America and the South Seas.[17]

The story of the Welsh revival is astounding. Begun with prayer meetings of less than a score of intercessors, then it burst its bounds and the churches of Wales were crowded for more than two years. One hundred thousand outsiders were converted and added to the churches, the vast majority remaining true to the end.

Drunkenness was immediately cut in half and many taverns went bankrupt. Crime was so diminished that judges were presented with white gloves, signifying that there were no cases of murder, assault, rape, robbery, or the like to consider. The police became unemployed in many districts.[18]

A report in a secular newspaper during the revival where a young man, Evan Roberts, was greatly used of God, read, "A wonderful revival is sweeping over Wales. The whole country, from the city to the coal mines underground is aflame with Gospel glory."

Wow! Stop and think for a moment what effect it would have on a nation if the daily newspapers, radio, television, and Internet had reports like that in this day and age. It happened before and God wants it to happen again. He longs to fulfill His promise for a global spiritual harvest. *"For as the earth brings forth its bud, as the garden causes the things that are sown in it to spring forth, so the Lord God **will** cause righteousness and praise to spring forth before **all the nations**"* (Isaiah 61:11).

- **Nothing will promote the cause of world missionary enterprises like revival in the Church.**

The closer we study the history of revivals the more we find the history of missions. One of the main purposes of God's reviving His people is to give them a burdened heart for the lost and for them to be obedient to the Great Commission in Matthew 28:19-20.

In the late Dr. Edwin Orr's publication, *The Re-Study of Revival and Revivalism*, there are overwhelming evidences of this truth. He shares what happened during the second great awakening, between 1791 and 1798.

> This period of revival in the United Kingdom brought forth the British and Foreign Bible Society, the Religious Tract Society, the Baptist missionary Society, the London Missionary Society, and the Church Missionary Society, and a host of auxiliary agencies for evangelism. It produced also some significant social reform, even in wartime.[19]

Later in the book, Edwin Orr shares another account of the correlation between revival and missions.

> Revived Americans duplicated the formation of various evangelical associations in Britain, founding the American Bible Society, the American Tract Society, the American Board of Commissioners. For Foreign missions, the Foreign Mission of The American Baptists and society

after society. The order and extent of missionary organization reflected somewhat the degree of involvement of each denominational constituency in the Awakening.

There is no doubt that the general awakening of the 1790s and the 1800s, with its antecedents, was the prime factor in the extraordinary burst of missionary enthusiasm and social service, first in Britain, then in Europe and North America. Thomas Charles, whose zeal for God provoked the formation of the British and Foreign Bible Society, was a revivalist of first rank in Wales. George Burder, who urged the founding of the Religious Tract Society, was a leader in the prayer union for revival. William Carey, a founder and pioneer of the Baptist Missionary Society, was one of a group who set up in England the simultaneous prayer union that spread through evangelical Christendom and achieved its avowed purpose in the revival of religion and the extension of the Kingdom of Christ abroad. The London Missionary Society and the Church Missionary Society grew out of the prayers of other Free Church and Church of England evangelicals in the Awakening. Methodist missions came from the same source, as did other Scottish societies and the Church of Scotland missions. **The revival provided the dynamic.**[20]

- **Nothing will enable the Church to live more for eternity than revival.**

In revival, Heaven comes down and touches earth to such a degree that we gain a far greater understanding of the fact that our little bit of time here on earth is just preparation for the eons of time we will serve our Lord Jesus in eternity.

This time on earth is just the testing time for God to see how much with which we can be trusted in the long haul of eternity. We will only understand the responsibility of God's people, the Church, in relation to the nations of the world now, when we understand the responsibility and privilege for which God is preparing the Church in the future. He is preparing His Church to share with Him, as His Bride, His sovereign power and authority over His eternal kingdom.

> *"Then the sovereignty, power and greatness of the kingdoms under the whole heaven will be handed over to the saints, the people of the Most High. His kingdom will be an everlasting kingdom, and all rulers will worship and obey Him"* (Daniel 7:27).
>
> *"To him who overcomes and does My will to the end, I will give authority over nations"* (Revelation 2:26).

When Paul wrote to the Ephesians, he was trying to get them to see the big picture: *"I pray that your hearts will be flooded with light so that you can see something of the future He has called you to share"* (Ephesians 1:18 TLB).

How revival drastically alters our perspectives is illustrated in the following abbreviated report, which was given by Boston Stone, a Presbyterian minister. It relates to a four-day extended observance of the Lord's Supper as multitudes came together from Kentucky State in 1800.

> The scene baffled description. Very many fell down as men slain in battle and continued for hours together in a...motionless state; sometimes for a few minutes...exhibiting signs of life by a...deep groan or a piercing shriek, or by a prayer for mercy, fervently uttered. After lying there for hours...they would rise shouting deliverance.... With astonishment did I hear men, women and children declaring the wonderful works of God.[21]

Another abbreviated report on the same camp meeting is given by Lewis Drummond in his book, *The Awakening That Must Happen*:

> No person seemed to wish to go home...hunger and sleep seemed to affect nobody—eternal things were the

vast concerns…. [People] who had [taken communion] for many years were now laying prostrate on the ground, crying out… "Oh how I would have despised any person a few days ago who would have acted as I am doing now"…. Persons of every description, white and black…in every part of the multitude were crying out for mercy in the most extreme distress.[22]

Do eternal issues grip our hearts and minds, influence our perspectives, and determine our priorities?

- **Sustained, genuine revival and spiritual awakening changes the course of history globally and hastens the day more than any other factor when we shall hear what John predicted:**

  "And there were loud voices in Heaven saying, 'The kingdoms of this world have become the kingdoms of our Lord and His Christ, and He shall reign forever and ever'" (Revelation 11:15).

Edwin Orr's research tells us that from the Awakening of 1792 onwards:

Some contemporaries claimed that there was unbroken revival for fifty years, until 1842 or thereabouts. It is true that there was no major recession in all that time, but there is evidence that another outpouring of the Spirit occurred in the United States in 1830, recognized as such, and that there were revivals in other countries in Europe and far afield in the 1830s and 40s. So it could be said that the Awakening of 1792 onwards lasted more than thirty years, and without a serious recession, was followed by another movement which lasted a dozen years and was then succeeded by a decade of definite decline.[23]

SECTION FIVE

THE PRICE FOR REVIVAL FIRE

The price for revival fire starts with having a vision for it and understanding our desperate need for it. It means that we have an understanding of the characteristics of revival from God's perspective—first from studying revivals in His Word, then from reading the historical accounts of subsequent revivals.

This knowledge then fuels the fire of a God-given burden for revival, making it a priority prayer request. It means we become *desperate* for God's hand to be moved in revival fire, first upon His people, and then in spiritual awakening among the lost. That means we become desperate intercessors who are convinced that real revival is the only hope to meet our desperate needs as the Body of Christ and in our violent, depraved world hurtling head-on for destruction. It's revival for survival.

In Isaiah 59:19 God tells us that, *"When the enemy comes in, like a flood the Lord will raise up a standard against him."*

The enemy has come in with such an unbelievable, inconceivable, horrendous flood of unprecedented filth, that it's going to take the *"standard"* of a titanic tidal wave of gigantic Holy Spirit proportions to knock him down and drown him out.

When the Body of Christ throws off its garments of lethargy and complacency and stirs itself up before God in united, diligent, determined prayer, God will show us how willing He is to fulfill His promises.

> *"Ask rain from the Lord in the season of the spring rain from the Lord who makes the storm clouds, who gives us showers of rain"* (Zechariah 10:1). *"For Zion's sake* [that means God's people] *I will not keep silent. And for Jerusalem's sake I will not remain quiet, till her righteousness shines out like the dawn, her salvation like a blazing torch"* (Isaiah 62:1 NIV).

Supernaturally Directed and Energized Praying

Now, the righteousness of the people of God will only shine out like the dawn when we deal seriously, through repentance, with everything in us that is unrighteous. Only as the Holy Spirit prays through our cleansed, surrendered, Spirit-controlled lives, will we have power in prayer. Revival praying is totally supernatural. I see a parallel between this kind of intercession and what happened to Mary when the angel told her that something was going to take place within her body that would defy any natural explanation. The answer to her legitimate question of *"How can this thing be?"* was dead simple. *"The Holy Spirit shall come upon you."* In humility and faith, her response was equally uncomplicated. *"Be it unto me according to Your word"* (Genesis 30:34).

We must first of all surrender our wills to God in the place of intercession. Then, we need to ask the Holy Spirit to convict us of any un-dealt-with sin, and wait in His presence. If conviction comes (and at times it has, to me), we need to repent and make any necessary restitution God may require.

Only then are we able to ask for, and by faith receive, the oncoming of the Holy Spirit to direct and energize us to pray for others. I am as convinced as the angel and Mary were, that without the enabling power of the Holy Spirit, the miraculous doesn't happen. When we have heard the Holy Spirit's direction, we simply speak that out in faith. We may need to wait until He gives that direction. Many times I have had to. But, oh the rewards!

Powerful, effective intercession that moves God's hand is always miraculous, because it's God at work through a yielded, clean, Spirit-controlled, obedient vessel with no agenda but His. The maximum effectiveness in prayer meetings is seldom realized because we fail to wait on God before we open our mouths. We have our agenda, our preconceived way of praying and our allotted time. God have mercy on us!

Having Only God's Agenda

One of the things God does in revival is to throw over our neatly planned, well-organized, and controlled agendas and show us what it's like when He's completely in charge. Believe me, there's a world of difference!

One of the greatest hindrances to the answers to our prayers for revival is that we don't give God *time* to work. Period. We pray for God's Spirit to break forth in power, but we definitely don't want Him to do it after 1 P.M. on Sundays, or after 9 P.M. any evening. Every sustained, deep outpouring of the Holy Spirit I've been in (and I've been in some remarkable ones) has *always* occurred when the clock was not the controlling factor.

For those who have understandable pastoral responsibilities related to people who are looking after children in church nurseries, is it not a matter of releasing those in the audiences who need to go and take care of their children? In this way, the rest of God's people are not denied the opportunity of experiencing the maximum measure of God's manifest presence on God's terms and His timetable.

One of the most superlative promises in God's Word is directed toward those who will learn the discipline of waiting on Him. *"For since the beginning of the world men have not heard nor perceived by the ear, nor has the eye seen any god besides You who acts for the one who waits for Him"* (Isaiah 64:4).

So many Christians and churches know so little, if anything, of what this means experientially. The most thrilling thing, along with winning people to Jesus, is to experience the strong manifest presence of the Lord. So many times He withholds that wonder because we don't have the spiritual ambition, humility, and patience to wait on His Majesty.

We don't have to try to twist God's arm to get Him to display His glory. But we do need to realign ourselves up to the ways of His Spirit from His Word. And that's going to take a lot of painful but essential adjustments from chiropractor God.

Just how desperate are we for God's revival fires to burn in our nation, our cities, our churches, or wherever else people meet? I can tell you for certain that preaching alone won't do it, no matter how full of truth or how powerful it is.

In the book, *Finney Lives On*, Raymond Edman shares these poignant quotes from Finney's teaching concerning the absolute necessity of prevailing intercession for divine intervention.

> Prayer is an essential link in the chain of causes that lead to a revival; as much so as truth is. Some have zealously used truth to convert men, and laid very little stress on prayer. They have preached, and talked, and distributed tracts with great zeal, and then wondered that they had

so little success. And the reason was, that they forgot to use the other branch of the means, effectual prayer. They overlooked the fact that truth by itself will never produce the effect without the Spirit of God; and the Spirit is given in answer to earnest prayer. Sometimes it happens that those who are the most engaged in employing truth are not the most engaged in prayer. This is always unfortunate—for unless they, or somebody else, have the spirit of prayer, the truth by itself will do nothing but harden men in impenitence. Probably in the day of judgment it will be found that nothing is ever done by the truth, used ever so zealously, unless there is a spirit of prayer somewhere in the connection with the presentation of truth.[24]

God has shaped history around His Church and He expects His Church to shape the history of the nations. Therefore all revival praying should start with a burdened heart for the Body of Christ in every nation. The present state of the Church alone should be enough to make us desperate in prayer.

It has amazed and grieved me to discover that there are actually parts of Christ's Body who don't believe other parts are even in the Body! Other segments of the Church only tolerate other segments and consequently are uncomfortable worshiping with or working together with them.

One of the most appalling discoveries is that the closer we get to many denominations, we find that each one is convinced that they have all the truth. I'm convinced that no group of people or any individual has all the truth, simply because there's no group or person humble enough to handle it. God in His wisdom keeps it that way in the hope that we will all have the humility of seeing our need to learn from each other. The reality is that the more God reveals to us of His character and ways, the more we realize how little we really know and how much we have yet to learn.

I love the stanza in a Baptist church hymnal that concluded every verse of a hymn I used to sing, which said, "There is yet more life and truth to spring forth from God's word." I want to add, *"Amen, Selah."*

It often takes severe persecution to the Body of Christ for us all to realize how desperately we need each other, whereas genuine humility would allow us to see how much we need to support and encourage as well as to learn from each other in freedom. So many times we're a laughingstock to the world because of so much disunity and hypocrisy.

A Desperate Remnant

We need to get desperate in prayer for revival because of the spirit of the world that invades the Church so that it is almost unrecognizable from the world in lifestyle, conversation, and values.

Millions of so-called born-again Christians have never won a soul to Christ, and there are millions more who seldom, if ever, witness to non-Christians. Millions of Christians have never done a thing about being obedient to the Great Commission in Matthew 28:19-20.

Only a Heaven-sent, Christ-centered, and Christ-exalting, Holy Spirit convicting deluge of the Spirit will cause us to be humble, desperate seekers of Him who alone is truth, with a passion for His manifest presence and glory. I have hope and faith for this because God never shares with us His burdens and the accompanying grace to sustain them, in order to frustrate us, only to fulfill us. God rewards diligent seekers (see Hebrews 11:6). But God waits for our desperate prayers. *"And there is no one who calls on Your name, who stirs himself up to take hold of You"* (Isaiah 64:7).

Ezra is a man who took that challenge from God, and showed by his response that he meant business by responding to it in iden-tificational repentance.

> *"At the evening sacrifice I arose from my fasting; and having torn my garment and my robe, I fell on my knees and spread out my hands to the Lord my God. And I said, "O my God, I am too ashamed and humiliated to lift up my face to You, my God; for our iniquities have risen higher than our heads, and our guilt has grown up to the Heavens"* (Ezra 9:5-6).

In the following nine verses Ezra continues to humble him-self before God in desperate intercession.

In verse 15 we find an encouraging key to those who are committed to taking up God's challenge as mentioned in Isaiah 64:7. Ezra prays. *"O Lord God...You are righteous, **for we are left as a remnant** as at this day. Here we are before You, in our guilt"* (Ezra 9:15). God has always had a remnant with whom He can work to change the course of history by their being obe-dient to His priorities. *"Even so then, at this present time there is a remnant according to the election of grace"* (Romans 11:5).

If ever there was a time in the history of America when God's remnant needs to cry out as David did in Psalm 119:126, it is now: *"It is time for You to act O Lord for* [we] *have regarded Your law as void."* Every major problem we are facing in the United States comes from our blatant rejection of the standards of God's holy Word, the Bible.

Have you noticed that desperate people are never self-con-scious? Listen to the following impassioned prayer from the young prophet Jeremiah who was a seasoned intercessor, calling us to have God's heart for the needy: *"The hearts of the people cry out to the Lord...let your tears flow like a river day and night; give yourself no relief, your eyes no rest. Arise, cry out in the night...pour out your heart like water, in the presence of the Lord...*" (Lamentations 2:18-19).

We've never been deep in prayer until we've become desperate for God's hand to be moved. Desperate people pray with diligence and determination while there's breath in their bodies, and until God answers.

I will illustrate from the life of Marie Monson who was a single Norwegian woman, sent by God to be a missionary in China. I am quoting from a book called *The Awakening*, which recounts the revival in China from 1927–1937. Marie Monson writes:

> We heard of the revival in Korea which began in 1907. It was a mighty movement and had been born through a prayer-revival among missionaries. Oh, to be able to go there and bring back some of the glowing coals to our own field! But the journey was long and expensive and I had not the money. As I prayed for money and looked for an answer, a definite word was sent instead: "What you want through that journey may be given here, where you are, in answer to prayer." The words were a tremendous challenge. I gave my solemn promise: "Then I will pray until I receive."[25]

Determined to Pay the Price

> Having pledged myself, I set out to cross the floor of my room to my place of prayer, in order to pray this prayer for revival for the first time. I had not taken more than two or three steps before I was halted. What then happened can only be described as follows: it was as though a boa constrictor had wound its coils around my body and was squeezing the life out of me. I was terrified. Finally, while gasping for breath, I uttered the one word, "Jesus! Jesus! Jesus! Jesus!" Each time I spoke out the precious Name, it grew easier to breathe, and in the end

the serpent left me; I stood there dazed. The first conscious thought was: "Then prayer means as much as that, and that my promise should be kept means as much as that." That experience helped me to endure through the almost twenty years which were to pass before the first small beginnings of revival were visible. Truly God works unhurriedly.[26]

Later, in her report, Marie Monson shared that "the burden of prayer was heavy upon me. There had been times on the field (for instance when traveling with fellow missionaries) when the burden was so great that I had to withdraw from the general conversation, in order to concentrate inwardly in silent prayer."[27]

A God-given burden for revival is a fire within your spirit ignited by the Holy Spirit that burns incessantly and is refueled every time you pray for it. *"I will kindle a fire in you and the blazing flame shall not be quenched"* (Ezekiel 20:47). This is one thing we cannot organize—it has to be agonized! Revival praying inevitably means going deeper in intercession because we're praying for the deepest thing to happen.

When Elijah prayed a one-sentence prayer on Mount Carmel, fire fell from Heaven. That was a sign and a wonder. But it took desperate, determined, diligent, travailing intercession before God sent the rain, which is a sign of the outpouring of the Holy Spirit. It means asking God for a revolution of righteousness to invade the Church and overflow out to the unconverted.

I love using the powerful prayer in Psalm 45:3-4: *"Gird Your sword upon Your thigh, O Mighty One, with Your glory and Your majesty. And in Your majesty ride prosperously because of truth, humility and righteousness; and Your right hand shall teach You awesome things."*

In Isaiah 66:7, God also likens it to the conception of a child in a mother's womb. As the mother eats the right foods, the baby is nourished and grows. We ask God to conceive the burden in us by His Spirit and release faith, and start praying for revival. We keep feeding the burden by keeping on praying for it. God makes it grow until it affects all our thinking, planning, preaching, and living. We're consumed with the vision and the burden to see it fulfilled.

In Isaiah 66:7-9 God tells us that when we get desperate enough to allow Him to travail in prayer through us (which often includes weeping and groaning), we can be assured the answers are on the way for an outpouring of His Spirit—rain from the Throne Room. "*As soon as Zion was in labor she brought forth her sons.*" Zion, means the people of God. So God is saying that when the Body of Christ gets this serious, not just some seasoned intercessors, then revival will be birthed.

He also tells us that we won't have a stillborn child. There will be fulfillment. "*Shall I bring to the birth and not cause to bring forth? Says the Lord; shall I, Who cause to bring forth, shut the womb? Says your God*" (Isaiah 66:9). And it always starts with the Church.

Marie Monson further reports:

It was a never-to-be-forgotten day, when the desire of twenty-three years was granted, and I stood at last in the room—the very crucible—where missionaries had met daily to pray. Here they were, stripped of all that was of self, till they were "unprofitable servants" in their own eyes and "declared themselves bankrupt." Here they unitedly resolved to continue in prayer until they were given a revival like the revival in India and in Wales. Their request was granted.[28]

As we pray all the prayers for revival from the prophets of God in the Word and sense their intensity, it helps our intensity. One of my favorite revival prayers in this category, and subsequent answers, is in Habakkuk 3:1-7. God has used it to inspire me and has encouraged me to use it in intercession on numerous occasions. The prophet Habakkuk, simply but with intensity, says to God, *"Lord, I have heard of Your fame; I stand in awe of Your deeds, O Lord. Renew them in our day, in our time make them known; in wrath remember mercy."*

This is how I interpret and use that prayer for worldwide revival:
Dear Father God, as You know, I have been studying revivals and revival praying in Your Word for decades; and avidly reading everything I could get my hands on about subsequent revivals; asking questions and learning from those who have been in revival; and praying fervently and frequently in faith for nearly 50 years for it. As a result, I am awestruck at who You are and how You work. It makes me tremble before You and experience the fear of the Lord at a deep level.

*On the other hand, it deeply inspires me to keep on asking You with boldness and childlike expectation to show up, and show off, **big time**, in my generation. Let this world see what You're really like, because they don't really have a clue how magnanimous and magnificent and magnetic and monumental and majestic and miraculous and meek and merciful You really are.*

*Come on God, do some of Your breathtaking, really big stuff that only You can do **now** because I'm getting weary of always hearing about it in the past. Please bring the revival scene up to date in the twenty-first century. Only then, we the Church will have a chance of repenting of our pride that we have chosen to live by any other standards than what You came to model for us, as Son of man.*

Because we can't repent of what we cannot see or sense, we so desperately need the outpoured Holy Spirit to come in revelation of our hearts as only You know them, and bring the depth of conviction that motivates us to have a change of life. Only the Holy Spirit, in revival can enable us, Your Church, to choose to make Christlikeness our goal and enable us to fulfill it. Only the flame of the Holy Spirit can ignite our hearts with Your love for a world hurtling toward hell, and motivate us to get out of our comfort zones and get involved in bringing them to Jesus.

Now, because You have graciously revealed to me something of what we may expect when You justifiably display all Your attributes, I plead with You to have mercy on us. I recall reading from Your Word that You are a great and terrible God, as well as one of unending mercy. Because of the mind-boggling display of Yourself and ways as a result of Habakkuk's prayer, I am daring to believe that because the need of this generation is millions times greater than in Habakkuk's day You will answer the cries of my heart for Your glory alone, and do something greater than in his day.

In Jesus' name and for the sake of the incredible price He paid on the cross to redeem mankind. Amen.

The Bible describes how the prophet Habakkuk's prayer was answered in verses 3-15:

God came from Teman, the holy One from Mount Paran [v. 3; Holiness].

His glory covered the heavens, and the earth was full of His praises [Glory].

His brightness was like the light [v.4; Brilliance].

He had rays flashing from His hands and there His power was hidden [Spectacular Power].

Before Him went pestilence and fever followed at His feet [v. 5; Judgment].

He stood and measured the earth; He looked and startled the nations, and the everlasting mountains were scattered. The perpetual hills bowed.
The sun and the moon stood still in their habitation [v. 11].
At the light of Your arrows they went, as the shining of Your glittering spear [Earthshaking Awesome Power].
You marched through the land in indignation, You trampled the nations in anger [v. 12; Wrath].
You went forth for the salvation of Your people, for salvation with Your anointed [v. 13; Deliverance].
His ways are everlasting [v. 6; Eternal].

The effect on the prophet Habakkuk was as follows: *"When I heard, my body trembled; my lips quivered at the voice; rottenness entered my bones; and I trembled in myself, that I may rest in the day of trouble when He comes up to His people, He will invade them with His troops"* (v. 16).

Revival is very awesome. The unleashing of the Holy Spirit is no light matter. Why should God send revival to casual Christians who know nothing about intense, regular, persistent prayer for it? The record is, He doesn't. Do you only pray for revival when others call you to, or are you known as one who, as a way of life, calls others to pray for it, until God answers?

The Humility Test

We need to be willing to be identified with **all** of God's children regardless of how they react to revival or act in revival. *"To the church of God which is at Corinth, to those sanctified in Christ Jesus, called to be saints together with **all those who in every place** call on the name of our Lord Jesus Christ, **both their Lord and ours**"* (1 Corinthians 1:2).

Only those who really fear the Lord and understand His character and His ways, who long to be part of the genuine deep moves of His Spirit, are the ones who ***don't*** fear the unusual or the unexpected. They've been walking in obedience to His promptings, which has included the unusual many times. Those people love to be identified with the real thing, even if it is unusual—especially when they're with people they know well and have learned to trust their character.

The question is, are we prepared to be identified with God's outpoured Spirit among those who don't come into that category? Would we respond to God and go among them and be a part of what He is doing? Are we prepared to be identified with them now?

In the outpouring of the Holy Spirit, all kinds of things surface that are otherwise hidden. Some examples are: uncrucified flesh in people who take advantage of the unusual and the unstructured, which marks revivals, by fleshly displays of excessive emotion; or, manifestations of demonic spirits, trying to get attention to divert and disrupt the work of the Holy Spirit.

God is going to work with and be identified with all this. Are we? We don't have to condone it and if we're in spiritual leadership we need to be prepared to gently deal with it in correction. When we pray for rain we can expect some mud!

Have we come to the place where we have chosen to have *no reputation*? It means being prepared to be nothing in any given situation that He may be everything. It means being like Jesus, who is the friend of every one of His children, who loves them unconditionally, works with them, and identifies with them.

Are our reserves about being identified with all of God's people really coming from a concern about our own reputation when we say it's His reputation we're concerned with? God is well able to look after His reputation.

Are we willing to be misunderstood, misjudged, and maligned by other Christians who choose not to be identified with the genuine moves of God's Spirit where unusual manifestations occur?

In the first great revival in the early Church (in the Book of the Acts) we read that the people who witnessed it said, *"These people must be drunk."* This proves the truth of First Corinthians 2:14: *"The natural man does not receive the things of the Spirit of God, for they are foolishness to him, neither can he know them for they are spiritually discerned."*

Then God goes on to say that we can trust Him to give us the spiritual discernment to know what things are of Himself. *"But he who is **spiritual**, judges all things..."* (1 Corinthians 2:15). We're all only as spiritual as we are Christlike, because that's our ultimate goal. And Jesus epitomizes humility.

Unity in the Body of Christ is essential for God's approving presence at all times. Psalm 133:3 tells us that God commands the blessing when we're united. God also says in Matthew 12:25 that we're only as strong as we are united. *"Every kingdom divided against itself is laid waste and no city or house divided against itself will stand."*

Isn't it strange therefore, that large amounts of time, energy, and money are utilized in preparation for so many Christian events, large or small, with relatively little time given to the one thing God says is a prerequisite for His showing up? Amazing!

Without unity in the Body of Christ, revival cannot be contained or sustained. Therefore it is an essential preparatory component for the deluge of the rain of the Holy Spirit for which we pray.

Unity in the Body of Christ will only be experienced when we understand what it means from the divine perspective. The standard of this unity is uniquely found in John, chapter 17, where Jesus prays that "*they may be one even as We are one.*" Therefore, Bible unity, is nothing less that Trinity unity—the unity that the Father and the Son and the Holy Spirit experience at all times.

We need to know what Their relationships are like because that is what we're supposed to be experiencing down here on earth.

Some of the Characteristics of the Relationship of the Trinity

- They are equal in authority but different in function.
- They complete each other in ministry function, never compete. Often we're not aware where one starts and another ends. There is a total blending of the three.
- They are totally dependent on each other, based on the humility which knows they desperately need each other.
- They have absolute truth in their relationships and therefore absolute trust.
- They support one another and serve one another.
- They have singleness of purpose.
- They have absolute holiness in their relationships, therefore experience the ultimate in enjoyment of one another.
- They are an invincible team who has an eternal, indestructible Kingdom, therefore the ultimate in effectiveness.

From Jesus' prayer in John 17:23, we understand that this Trinity unity is a powerfully convincing proof to the world of the following two things:

1. That God the Father sent God the Son to the earth in the person of the Lord Jesus Christ.
2. That God the Father loves His disciples on earth today equally as He loves His Son.

That means, unity in the Body of Christ absolutely, irrevocably convinces the world of the Deity of the Lord Jesus Christ and the total commitment of the Godhead to every disciple of the Lord Jesus.

The power and force of this unity cannot be hidden. It is glowingly obvious to the non-Christian. The source of it is the same glory that God the Father gave to His Son, and it shines through them according to John 17:22: *"And the glory which You have given Me, I have given to them; that they may be one, even as We are one."* This, in turn, strongly motivates the non-Christian to commit his life to the Lord Jesus Christ.

In Acts, chapter 2, unity and prevailing, persistent prayer, coupled with the preaching of the Word of the Lord with authority, set the stage for the outpouring of the Holy Spirit. This resulted in 3,000 people being converted and baptized in one day.

God's ways have not changed. First, we need unity of heart with God. That means we embrace His absolute justice, faithfulness and lovingkindness, regardless of our circumstances. *"He is the Rock, His work is perfect: For all His ways are justice, a God of truth and without injustice: righteous and upright is He"* (Deuteronomy 32:4).

The Price for Biblical Unity

Then we need unity of heart with every other person. And we're only as united as we're free from reserves in our hearts. A reserve, unchecked, will produce coldness, aloofness, resentment, judging, criticism, lack of confidence, lack of fellowship, lack of love, and disunity. A reserve is less than *"loving one another with a pure heart, fervently"* (1 Peter 1:22). The Greek word for "fervently" literally means "boiling point." It is essential that we do everything within our power to be reconciled to everyone where needed.

There are several imperative injunctions from God's Word in relation to this. *"Therefore confess your trespasses to one another and pray for one another, that you may be healed"* (James 5:16).

In Matthew 5:23-24, Jesus tells us that if we know that someone has something against us, we must go to that person to seek reconciliation. And in Matthew 18:15, Jesus says that if someone sins against us, we are to go and tell him his fault alone. The Bible also tells us that we are to speak the truth in love, gentleness, and humility. Finally, Colossians 3:13 (NIV) says, *"Bear with each other and forgive whatever grievances you may have against one another. Forgive as the Lord forgave you."*

It is also very important that we are united in our understanding of the ways of the Holy Spirit in revival. We must be willing to see the truth from God's Word about fulfilling the command to be filled with the Holy Spirit as in Ephesians 5:18. We must be equally willing to allow the Holy Spirit to manifest Himself in whichever way He sovereignly chooses. Sadly, too often, through fear, pride, prejudice, or unbelief, we can close our minds and hearts to the full operation of the Holy Spirit in us and through us. And then we criticize others who do yield to Him and obey His promptings.

In revival, the reign of the Holy Spirit is outpoured as described in Zechariah 10:1 and Isaiah 44:3. We choose to either put up our umbrellas of resistance or invite God to soak us. It depends on how thirsty we are for His manifest presence.

As I have made an in-depth study of revivals for about 48 years, I have found they are characterized by terrible conviction, agonized cries and groans, wailing, uncontrollable sobbing, shaking, shouting, confessions, repentance, exuberant joy, praise, singing, testimonies, powerful preaching from the Word of God, prevailing, persistent prayer, a heavy burden for the lost, an increased hunger for the Word of God, a passionate love for the Lord Jesus, a great increase of the fear of the Lord, the clock doesn't dictate the agenda, a display of God's judgment to those who repeatedly resist the Holy Spirit's presence and power, God overthrowing men's agendas, unlikely people being used of God in powerful ways, unprecedented numbers of lost souls coming to Christ, and the cause of missions being greatly advanced—to name a few.

Unity among God's people is of such a priority to God as evidenced in Jesus' prayer in John 17, that at times He will actually hold back the answers to desperate prayers of intercessors praying for revival to break out. He sees that to answer them would bring major division because so many of the spiritual leaders and their followers have little or no understanding of the ways of the Spirit in revival.

So, God keeps encouraging His intercessors to keep on praying in faith for revival, while at the same time working to try and influence the resistant ones to His Spirit, to yield to Him and face the truth from His Word and the history of nation-changing revivals, and then go with God's flow. That's why revival praying must always start with having a burdened heart for His people, first—because that's where the blockage is.

Remember the familiar verse in First Chronicles 7:14? The first requisite God requires before He can heal any nation is to get His people to *humble* themselves and repent of all known sin. It's far easier for God to find people to pray (and that's never easy), than it is to find people who will humble themselves. That's because pride is by far our greatest sin, and humility is our greatest need. Pride doesn't last long in revival. Humility thrives on it. Because revival is God having center stage in His way and in His timing, doing His incredible thing! And man is definitely in the wings, and at best, backstage.

If that's what you yearn and burn with desire for, you'll be willing to fulfill the conditions laid out in the rest of this section of this book.

God will not be able to trust His people with revival and spiritual awakening until we are reconciled and functioning in unity, in gender, racially, denominationally, and generationally. Only the Holy Spirit can reveal the pride and prejudices that still linger. We can glibly say we're all in unity, but our actions have yet to fully match our words in all those arenas.

Because God has brought His people a long way in recent years in this regard, we can trust Him to complete His work. Our part is to keep praying until there is equality on God's terms, found in His Word. We partner with the Lord Jesus as we do so.

Further Preparation for Revival Fire

In revival we need to be prepared for the influx of thousands of new converts who need discipling. During the height of the revival that swept America from 1857–1858 when Charles Finney was being so mightily used of God, it was estimated that 50,000 conversions were occurring in a single week—without the help of radio, television, or the Internet. Think about that!

If we think we're too involved in Christian service now, all I can say is, "We haven't seen anything yet." The prophet Jeremiah asks these relevant, pertinent questions. *"If you have run with the footmen, and they have wearied you, then how can you contend with horses? And if in the land of peace, in which you trusted, they wearied you, then how will you do in the floodplains of the Jordan?"* We can always be assured that God's supernatural enabling power and grace are always available to every one of His servants who is doing His will in His way and time.

A word of warning is needed here. It is of the utmost importance that we understand the need to personally maintain God's priorities on a daily basis when everything of eternal purposes is being accelerated, as in revival. We cannot afford to neglect the following:

- Our times of personal worship
- Time in the Word of God
- Waiting on God for directions and wisdom
- Intercession
- Personal witnessing

We must be operating in the love of God and fulfilling the conditions to be empowered by the Holy Spirit at all times.

It is also important that, if you are a spiritual leader, you don't deprive your people of having regular times for having their "spiritual batteries" recharged through worship, intercession, and being fed from God's Word, at the price of all the time and energies being poured into the more spectacular side of the ministry in evangelism.

One of the features of all revivals is the number of spiritual leaders and professing Christians who get converted. It was so under Charles Finney's preaching. It was also the case for the China revival of 1927–1937, as Marie Monson has reported:

> Some [of the American missionaries] were saved in the revival....Some came through into salvation after holding out obstinately against the Spirit of God. Some chose to go back to America rather than be saved. The contrast between themselves and the newly saved missionaries was too obvious and too great for them to be able to enjoy working under the new conditions revival had created.[29]

This Norwegian missionary gave a further report.

There was the pastor who stood banging the floor with his stick with rage, and who really looked as though he very much wished he could chastise the person who had dared to say that even a pastor might be unsaved. One day while he was walking along a muddy street, he was so overpowered by the Spirit of God that he fell down on his hands and knees in the road, crying out for mercy.[30]

We also need to ask God to prepare us for the price of ministering to people who have been exposed to the awesome holiness of God, which produces the revelation of their sin as God sees it. In the revival in China, Marie Monson shares a graphic description of this price, which has deeply impacted me. She writes:

After very busy days, over and over again half the night too would be spent in helping sick souls. Such work is costly and difficult because conviction of sin can be so overwhelming, and the confessions made were at times so horrible that even strong men missionaries preferred to be spared a share in this side of the work. It carried them to the gates of hell and brought sleepless nights. But this messenger of God never pitied herself through these long years. She had been entrusted with a holy, God-given ministry and it was to her His gift of grace.[31]

If we're in positions of spiritual leadership we need to give God 100-percent honest answers to these questions:

1. Am I really willing to pay the price to lead in the outpouring of the Spirit where the unusual is normal?

2. Have I a conscious, or perhaps subconscious, preference to be in control of situations, or for others to be in control when the unpredictable and unusual breaks out?

3. Am I controlled by the fear of man or the fear of the Lord?

4. Am I willing to take the responsibility of trusting and obeying the promptings of the Holy Spirit for direction to know if I am not to hinder people engaging in unusual manifestations, or to gently but firmly correct them?
5. Am I willing to submit to a God-given plurality of spiritually sensitive, mature leaders during such times, regardless of gender or race?

A characteristic of revival is for God to bypass the normal programs and timetables of men. For those who are uncomfortable with that scenario, be encouraged by the following report from Edwin Orr's book, *Evangelical Awakenings During 1900*: "The outstanding feature of the Welsh revival was utter spontaneity. The understandable fear of the ministers that the meetings would get out of control was met by the trust that the Spirit moving the people would rebuke deviation."[32]

This point of trusting God in this way is wonderfully illustrated in the following report by Charles Finney, out of the book, *Finney Lives On*.

I have said that this work began in the Spring of 1829. In the Spring of 1831, I was at Auburn again. Two or three men from this lumber region came there to see me, and to enquire how they could get some ministers to go in there. They said that not less than five thousand people had been converted in that lumber region; that the revival had extended itself along for eighty miles, and there was not a single minister of the gospel there.

I have never been in that region; but from all I have ever heard about it, I have regarded that as one of the most remarkable revivals that have occurred in this country. It was carried on almost independently of the ministry, among a class of people very ignorant in regard to all ordinary instruction; and yet so clear and wonderful were the teachings of God that I have always understood the revival was remarkably free from fanaticism, or wildness, or anything that was objectionable.[33]

To help readers understand the implications that are involved with the answers to the former questions, I am going to share with you an account of what happened to Rev. Ivor Davies. He was a Presbyterian senior missionary in the Congo in the 1950s, who had been praying for revival, with other missionaries for many months. God answered, initially by pouring out His Spirit, first of all on the nationals on a mission compound in another area, where unusual manifestations occurred amongst them.

In the little book, *This Is That*, published by The Christian Literature Crusade, an account is given by Ivor Davies as follows:

We were out on trek when a letter reached us, telling us of these happenings. After I read it, I got a vision from the Lord of what was going to happen. I saw the meetings with the people shouting, shaking, and making confession—all the manifestations which we have later seen. The vision shook me, and I got a fear of the whole thing. My own inability brought a fear, as I knew the people would crowd to me for help, and a great longing came to run away from it all; but I prayed to the Lord to help me, and came through willing to be used. It was one thing to pray for revival, quite another to be willing for it. Before returning to the station, I had another vision. A hard rock was standing up before me. I saw blood running over the face of it, and while I watched the blood congealed. I wondered at the vision, but did not understand it. When I got back, the thought came to me strongly to look up the meaning of the word "congealed" and I found, "Congealed is the state some liquids become when poured over a cold surface." Then I understood.[34]

The Holy Spirit said, "That rock is a picture of your hard, cold heart," and then He convicted him of the belittling way he spoke to his wife in front of the other missionaries, and then the belittling way he spoke to the African nationals. He deeply repented before God and made open restitution of all this to all the people.

Then, God showed him that the unusual things that he was seeing and hearing were of Himself as the nationals were obeying the promptings of the outpoured Holy Spirit. As a direct result of this senior missionary's brokenness, God faithfully released to him the wisdom that he needed to lead the people, in many unusual circumstances. *"When pride comes, then comes shame; but with the humble is wisdom"* (Proverbs 11:2).

There were unusual manifestations of the Holy Spirit that they came to call "fixations." There were times when people repeatedly resisted the convicting work of the Holy Spirit, only to find that their limbs would lock and they were unable to move them. For example, one of the national women who had been speaking a lot against one of the missionaries found herself unable to move from sitting on a low stool. Her legs seemed fixed and stuck to the ground, and she was crying pitifully in great distress. After being counseled by the leaders and her cooperating with them, release came. Only after she confessed and deeply repented of her sin of criticism was she able to move her legs and stand up again.

On other occasions, during the meetings, Ivor Davies would observe a few people with one arm in a locked position up in the air. Upon inquiry, he found that they were unable to bring it down, and at the same time were under a heavy burden of intercession for those who were resisting the Holy Spirit. As the travail in prayer continued, individuals would eventually call out from the audience, "I can't resist the Spirit any longer."

They would then name their sin and weep in brokenness before God in deep repentance. Immediately, the fixed limbs would unlock and the intercessors knew the purpose for the fixation was completed.

These are some of the ways of the Spirit. I had a similar experience while counseling a beautiful Christian girl in her teens, who was from a strong Christian home. She approached me after a meeting and asked me to seek God on her behalf as she was aware there was a blockage in her spiritual life but didn't know what it was. I knew her well and had an immediate witness in my spirit that God was in this encounter. I observed that the fingers and thumb on one of her hands were locked in a closed position, making her hand look like the claw of a hen. She said she had no explanation of this phenomenon. Immediately I knew it was a sign of the Holy Spirit's working and assured her not to worry but to be completely honest before God and me.

As I sought God, He said one word to me, "Unbelief." As I spoke it out, the Holy Spirit showed her that this sin was operating in her life by keeping her from witnessing to her high school friends about the reality of the Lord Jesus and what He meant to her. Immediately she humbled herself in open confession and deep repentance, her hand was released to its normal condition.

Jesus Is Our Model

Spiritual leaders have told me that they don't have the time for the priority that I believe the Bible shows us we're to give to the critically important ministry of intercession.

My answer is simply that Jesus is our role model. He not only came:

(a) To show us what the Father is like;

(b) To die upon the cross and make atonement for the sins of the world, for those who would appropriate that atonement;

(c) To defeat the powers of darkness by His death and resurrection;

but He came to show us:

(d) *How to live* and

(e) *To be our life.*

Jesus never spent more time ministering to people than He spent alone with the Father in fellowship and in prayer. He was seldom anywhere else but up the Mount of Olives when evening came. Prayer was such an obvious priority to Him.

Luke 5 describes Jesus in the midst of a day of heavy ministry happenings. Verse 16 says, *"But Jesus often withdrew to lonely places and prayed."* The literal translation is, "He was withdrawing and praying." Meaning, He did this as a way of life. Another time, after a power-packed day of teaching in the Synagogue and healing many who were sick and demon-possessed, as the whole city came to where He was, we read from Mark 1:35: *"Now in the morning having risen a long time before daylight, He went out and departed to a solitary place, and there He prayed."*

It is very significant that the one thing Jesus' disciples asked Him to teach them was how to pray. Obviously they concluded by His lifestyle that His prayer life was the secret of His effectiveness in ministry.

What a magnificent master and role model He is. What else, other than pride would motivate us to choose to live by standards other than His. It is little wonder that God exhorts us in Zephaniah 2:3 to "seek humility."

Since Jesus returned to Heaven, Hebrews 7:25 says the ministry of intercession is still a priority with Him: *"He always lives to make intercession for* [His own]."

For God's maximum purposes to be fulfilled in situations that relate to the extension of His Kingdom, He looks for spiritual leaders whom He can appoint and anoint. This is a principle throughout God's Word.

God not only desires to bring revival, but He needs spiritual leaders who have had the deep heart preparation needed to be used of Him when He sends it. Therefore, we should prioritize our prayers toward this section of the Church.

In Judges 5:2, we are assured that the people will follow when the appropriately prepared leaders take the lead. And Psalm 110:3 assures us that God's people will follow those leaders when His Spirit is poured out.

I wonder what the reaction would be of many spiritual leaders today if there was a reenactment by the Holy Spirit of what took place at the Cane Ridge revival in Bourbon county in the U.S.A. in 1801 when 20,000 people arrived for a six-day camp meeting. Mendell Taylor gives his eyewitness account in his book *Exploring Evangelism*:

> The noise was like the roar of Niagara. The vast sea of human beings seemed to be agitated as if by a storm. I counted seven ministers, all preaching at one time, some on stumps, others in wagons and one standing on a tree which had, in falling, lodged against another.... Some of the people were singing, others praying, some crying for mercy in the most piteous accents, while others were shouting most vociferously. While witnessing these scenes, a peculiarly strange sensation such as I had never felt before came over me. My heart beat tumultuously, my knees trembled, my lips quivered and I felt as if I must fall to the ground. A strange supernatural power seemed to pervade the entire mass of people there collected.... I stepped up on a log where I could have a better view of the surging sea of humanity. The

scene that then presented itself to my mind was inde-
scribable. At one time I saw at least five hundred swept
down in a moment as if a battery of a thousand guns
had been opened up on them and then immediately followed shrieks and shouts that rent the very heavens.[35]

God's Word is not silent about our need to tremble in His
holy presence, with the fear of the Lord upon us. *"Do you not
fear Me?" says the Lord. "Will you not tremble at My presence...? This is the one I esteem; he who is humble and contrite
in spirit and trembles at My Word"* (Isaiah 66:2 NIV). And, *"O
worship the Lord in the beauty of holiness! Tremble before
Him, all the earth"* (Psalm 96:9).

Praying for Spiritual Leaders

Dear reader, I don't think you would have come this far in
reading this book if you were not serious about spiritual things.
Therefore I am going to ask you to join with me in regularly interceding for the spiritual leaders of your nation, your city, your
church, and your Christian organization as follows:

1. Pray that God will give them a burdened heart for genuine revival, which will be evident by their prayer lives.
2. Pray that leaders would teach, inspire, and encourage
   others to have a burdened heart for revival from God's
   Word.
3. Pray that leaders would call their people to revival praying.
4. Pray that leaders will seek God for an understanding of
   the ways of the Spirit from God's Word and study about
   how God has worked in past revivals.
5. Pray that leaders will be sensitive and flexible, and will
   flow with whatever new thing God may want to do in
   any situation, regardless of their traditions and liturgies.
6. Pray that leaders will be taken over by the fear of the
   Lord and be released from the fear of men.

7. Pray that leaders will recognize that the fear of the Lord is the source of their much-needed wisdom.

8. Pray that the leaders will be given a desire to be radically real and to repent of all hypocrisy.

9. Pray that leaders will not be concerned for their personal reputation.

10. Pray that leaders will be prepared to move beyond their comfort zones and trust God to give them directions when the unusual and the unpredictable takes place.

11. Pray that they will have the humility to confer with others whom they know listen to and obey the Holy Spirit as a way of life, if they're not sure what to do, regardless of race or gender.

12. Pray that leaders will be prepared and ready to be used by God and sent anywhere by God at any time in revival.

For a more comprehensive in-depth teaching on how to pray for spiritual leaders, see Joy Dawson's book, *Intercession, Thrilling and Fulfilling*, chapter 10.

Revival Provokes Persecution

The greatest threat to satanic forces is the Church of Jesus Christ united in a pure fervent love for Himself and then for the lost. That really stirs the enemy into aggressive action. His main strategy is to paralyze God's people with fear and he'll go to any lengths to achieve that goal. What he keeps forgetting is that God's perfect love coming upon and operating through His children, overcomes those fear tactics, and our opposition is left confused and frustrated.

In 1999, the international ministry of Open Doors, led by Brother Andrew, published a small book about the genuine revival in Cuba that started in 1998.[36] The following stories are taken from that source and illustrate what I have just stated. As always, God's people had to pay the price beforehand in fervent, frequent, prevailing, united prayer before God unleashed His Spirit in the great spiritual awakening among the unconverted in that land.

Many times, God used demonstrations of His miracle-working power on peoples' bodies to bring the crowds to hear the preaching of the gospel. By 1991, conservative estimates suggest that the Church in Cuba had grown to over 1,000,000 believers strong. Today, estimates place the number of house churches at well over 10,000 and the other evangelical churches at approximately 1,200.

From the beginning of the house church movement, the communist authorities were afraid of it and inflicted every form of pressure, from harassment to forced closure. One pastor in Central Cuba had 2,000 coming regularly to his house church, which meant he had to address the congregation in the streets from the top of his flat-roofed garage. This resulted in the authorities arresting him in 1995. In one day he was tried, convicted, and sentenced to nearly two years of imprisonment with hard labor for "disobedience" and "illicit meetings."

When he had been previously ordered to close down his house church he said, "The doors of my house are open. I will never close down a church that Jesus has opened." Following a major prayer campaign around the world that was launched on his behalf, he was released after serving half his prison sentence. He testified of the strength and health he experienced in answer to many prayers and the many opportunities to share the gospel with other inmates. The prisoners asked him if he was in prison as a punishment from God, and he said, "No, God sent me here to share the love of Christ with you."

Another strong outspoken spiritual leader in Cuba was also a medical doctor and was falsely charged with being a C.I.A. agent, and imprisoned. He writes:

> I was unjustly shut away in a prison dungeon. There were days in which, for over sixteen hours at a time, they kept me in total darkness. I couldn't see my own hands. I was the

subject of intense interrogations as well as physical and mental torture. I was switched back and forth between a boiling hot sauna and a freezing cold room.

Another time they told me I was going to be executed by a firing squad. They let me hear screams of terror and then gunfire and showed me trails of blood that were splattered on the walls as they took me to the room where the soldiers were holding their rifle in position to fire at me. I responded, "God loves all of you! Jesus lives! Cuba for Christ!"

I heard the order, "Fire." Then came the click of triggers and the mocking laughter of the soldiers. It was a mock execution, as part of the mental torture. I kept repeating, "Cuba for Christ," which was the slogan throughout the spiritual awakening.[37]

Before his release, this spiritual leader experienced 47 days of interrogation and torture. After that he was put under house arrest and he and his family became targets of constant surveillance and threats by officials. All this only increased their love for the Lord and their deep desire and fervent intercession to see their country won for God.

Revival and spiritual awakening comes with a "price tag." Those who will pay the price are the overcomers God speaks about in the Book of Revelation, and to them He gives a crown of life. They will prove that God's rewards far outweigh the price to serve Him, and the privilege of suffering for His cause is infinitely higher than the price of suffering. After all, He's King God, creator and sustainer of the universe.

THE FIRE OF GOD IN JUDGMENT

Wе really don't have a passion for truth until we are prepared to study every aspect of God's character, which is the essence of truth. The character of God is like a huge, multi-faceted diamond. Only when a diamond expert puts that kind of a diamond under his special magnifying eyeglass is the true beauty and value of the stone discovered. He will turn the diamond around, carefully observing all the many different scintillating and fascinating facets. He scrutinizes it as only a professional in his field of expertise can. Only he can describe it with genuine authority.

Truth or Distortion

God has many facets to His infinitely more wonderful and exquisitely beautiful character, and it's only when we take the time to study them all, one by one, dodging none, will we ever be able to fully know Him as He really is, and effectively make Him known. If we major on studying only the parts of God's character that appeal to us the most and then emphasize them over and above His other character-istics in our teaching and sharing, we will inevitably be giving a dis-torted view of God to others.

I believe the most balanced view of God's character that is summed up in one verse of the Bible is found in Jeremiah 9:24: *"Let him who glories, glory in this, that he understands and knows Me, that I am the Lord, exercising loving kindness, judgment and righteousness in the earth. For in these I delight says the Lord."*

Loving-Kindness	Judgment	Righteousness
(longsuffering and merciful)	(justice)	(holiness)

So, God delights equally in displaying Himself in these three main attributes from which all His other attributes flow. When we major on any one of them more than another, we obviously have an unbalanced view of Him, which inevitably produces constant confusion or incorrect descriptions and explanations of Him.

From God's viewpoint, the subject of Himself as a God of Judgment is all too seldom spoken about today, and as a result many people are ignorant. *"But My people do not know the judgment of the Lord"* (Jeremiah 8:7).

In Jeremiah 5, God goes to great lengths to explain His justice when operating in judgment. I love the way God links the subject of His judgment with pursuing truth, when He tells His people to look everywhere and see if we can find anyone who *"executes judgment, who seeks truth"* (Jeremiah 5:1).

If we really want to know the truth about who God is, we must study and embrace His judgment equally along with His other attributes. It also means that when we have to exercise judgment we must be zealous to have all the facts before we do.

Then in Jeremiah 5, verses 4 and 5, God goes further and makes some rather startling statements about spiritual maturity and the lack of it: (1) People who don't understand the judgment of God are both foolish and don't know the way of the Lord. (2) Truly great men know both. Think about that. *"Therefore I said, Surely these are poor; they are foolish; for they don't know the way of the Lord, the judgment of their God. I will go to the great men and speak to them, for they have known the way of the Lord, the judgment of their God."*

I have studied and taught extensively from God's Word for many years on God's greatness, God's love, His holiness, His faithfulness, His mercy, His justice, His peace, the joy of the Lord, the glory of God, the power of God, the sovereignty of God, the understanding and tenderness of God as the lover of our souls. I cannot afford not to study and speak, and now write, on His judgment and wrath if I want to truly know Him and make Him known. And I do!

As the Lord Jesus was the express image of the Father, we study Jesus' life on earth to know what God is like. He manifested every attribute of God's character as Son of Man, including His judgment and wrath. Some examples are:

(1) When Jesus often vehemently confronted hypocrisy in the Pharisees.

(2) When trading in the Temple took priority over prayer, Jesus took a whip, overturned the moneychangers, and drove out those who bought and sold.

(3) When Jesus cursed the fig tree.

Understanding God's Justice Is Pivotal

Before we look into God's Word about the fire of God in judgment, I believe we need to stop and think about God's justice. Studying the justice of God has been one of the most rewarding biblical pursuits of my life. It has been pivotal to my search for the knowledge of God in order to make Him known. Further than that, I believe we will never understand God or His ways without studying His justice. At the same time, we discover that one of the most intriguing aspects of God's character is His incomprehensibility. As much as it is exciting to be on a journey of discovering as much as there is to know about God, I again stand in awe when He says *"that as far as the heavens are above the earth, so far are My thoughts and ways above yours"* (Isaiah

55:8). *"And My ways are past finding out"* (Romans 11:33). That mystery is a part of God's very Being; it puts Him in a class totally like no other.

I had already written most of this section on the fire of God's judgment, when I awoke one morning and, before rising, the Holy Spirit clearly instructed me to include a section on God's justice. I immediately understood why, because of what I have just shared.

God's righteous judgments for our sins were put upon Jesus at the cross. That punishment was willingly taken by our Savior as He became sin for us. God's judgment for sin was fully atoned for, by Jesus' shedding His blood at Calvary for all of us as sinners. Through our confession and repentance of our sinful nature and all its activities, we are completely forgiven by Him. Jesus cleanses us and gives us eternal life.

But we are all responsible for our ongoing thoughts, words, and actions, and will one day have to give an account of them to Jesus, to whom God has assigned the authority of all judgment: *"The Father...has given [Jesus] authority to execute judgment.... Because He is the Son of Man"* (John 5:26; Acts 10:42; 17:31). *"God will bring to judgment both the righteous and the wicked, for there will be a time for every activity, a time for every deed"* (Ecclesiastes 3:17).

Judgment Day for Christians

At the judgment seat of Christ, every born-again believer will be judged by what the Lord Jesus Christ has authorized to be written in the records about our lives from the vantage point of knowing and seeing everything. *"For there is **nothing** that is covered that will not be revealed, nor hidden that will not be known"* (Luke 12:2)—that means, every sin since our conversion, that we are aware of and have not repented of and made restitution for, as directed by the Holy Spirit. It means sins of omission as well as commission.

And the final test will be by the fire of God's judgment where our motives, words, and actions will be tried according to our privileges, opportunities, and potential. *"Each one's work will become clear, for the Day will declare it, because it will be revealed by fire; and the fire will test each one's work, of what sort it is"* (1 Corinthians 3:13).

The following will be disclosed:
- What we did that related to eternity and will last throughout eternity.
- What was done in obedience, solely to God's directions and in His timing—devoid of presumptions.
- What was done according to God's character and His ways, from His Word, (not necessarily the traditions, good ideas, liturgies, and schedules of men).
- What was done that brought glory to the Name of the Lord alone.

There is a solemn warning to all of us from First John 2:28: *"And now little children, abide in Him, so that when He shall appear, we may not be ashamed* [some translations say, "shrink back in terror"] *before Him at His coming."* True "abiding in Him" means that He becomes the only explanation of what happens spiritually in us and through us at all times. I call it desperate dependence and released faith. It's an unbeatable combination that produces fruit that remains and by which it is illogical, insane, and obnoxious to give anyone else the glory other than our magnificent Master, the Living Christ.

We need to keep linking together in our minds what God repeatedly links together in His Word: the judgments of God and the justice of God. *"Shall not the judge of all the earth do right?"* (Genesis 18:25)

God *"now commands all men everywhere to repent, because He has appointed a day on which He will judge the world in righteousness by the man whom He has ordained. He has given assurance of this to all by raising Him from the dead"* (Acts 17:30-31).

Our all-loving, infinitely understanding, deeply compassionate Heavenly Father yearns over His beloved children and asks us to do ourselves a favor by preparing ourselves for the Judgment Day. He doesn't want us to be embarrassed and ashamed and full of regrets. Listen to His cry: "*Therefore O* [My people] *I will judge you, each one according to his ways, declares the Sovereign Lord. Repent. Turn away from all your offenses; then* [unrepented] *sin will not be your downfall*" (Ezekiel 18:30 NIV).

God's Judgment on Man's Independence

One of the most awesome biblical accounts of the fire of God in judgment upon spiritual leaders is found in Leviticus 10:1-2. It contains lessons from which we all need to remind ourselves. We sing the song, "Our God is an awesome God who reigns in heaven above, in wisdom, power, and love. Our God is an awesome God." Do we really understand how His awesomeness can be displayed at times, through His judgments?

Nadab and Abihu were sons of Aaron and priests who had been sanctified and set apart by God for ministering to God and then to the people, in daily duties in the Temple. One day, their father Aaron had lifted his hands toward the people and blessed them, having just offered the sin offering, the burnt offering, and the peace offering to the Lord on behalf of the people. Everything was going according to God's plans with blessings abounding, and God decided to display His glory to everyone by sending fire down from Heaven which consumed the burnt offering and the fat on the altar, bypassing all human involvement. This was not your everyday occurrence, but a truly breathtaking encounter with Almightyness that caused them all to shout out loud and fall down flat on their faces on the ground.

However, by their subsequent actions, Nadab and Abihu were obviously not operating in the fear of the Lord and certainly didn't have the fear of God in their hearts. They decided to do their own thing by taking their censers and putting their own fire in them and then placing incense on them (without having any direction from the Lord to do so), manifesting the sins of independence and presumption. Both are based in pride.

God's reaction was immediate. No second chances. *"So fire went out from the Lord and devoured them, and they died before the Lord"* (Leviticus 10:2). God's Word calls it *"profane fire"* that they were bringing before the Lord. If the fire of the Holy Spirit's power is not what we're by faith receiving and depending upon when we're ministering to God and to others, we're not only useless, but we're giving a distorted view of God to people through our lack of authority in ministry. God doesn't anoint phoneys.

That's why God explained His acts of judgment to Moses by saying, *"'By those who come near me I must be regarded as holy; and before all the people I must be glorified.' So Aaron held his peace"* (Leviticus 10:3). Aaron got the message; that's why he was silent. There was nothing to defend.

An un-anointed servant of God distorts the character of God to the people. Those of us who minister are to *"speak as the oracles of God. If anyone ministers, let him do it with the ability which God supplies, that in all things God may be glorified"* (1 Peter 4:11). God can only be glorified when He's the only explanation of what comes through us; through our total submission, dependence, obedience, and faith.

We need to make sure we're fulfilling the following conditions for ministry, from God's perspective. We need to know we:
  (1) Are called of God to the ministry assignment we're in.
  (2) Are functioning in our God-given giftings and ministries, in joyful submission to the leadership to which God has assigned us.
  (3) Have a clean heart and a yielded will to God, motivated by love to Him and the people to whom we are serving.

(4) Are daily being empowered by the Holy Spirit with full understanding that we're utterly useless without Him.

(5) Are being obedient to revealed truth from God's Word and the promptings of the Holy Spirit.

(6) Are speaking only when and where He directs, the specific message He directs us to give from His Word, through seeking His face, and living each message as a way of life.

If, dear reader, you know you're honestly not fulfilling those conditions, why don't you thank God for His mercy for this wake-up call and tell Him you won't go on faking it in ministry; that you will become real? Ask God for the fire of His Spirit in conviction and purifying, and tell Him you're through with offering your own (profane) fire before the Lord. Then ask Him to drench you in His holy fire that enables and empowers you to represent Him to others as He really is. The more we investigate the subject of the fire of God in judgment, the more we see the need to take it seriously.

The fire of God consumed some of the Israelites because of their complaining and murmuring and was only stopped by Moses' intercession on their behalf (see Numbers 11:1-2). God's attitude toward the sin of complaining is the same today. It's obnoxious to Him. The antidote is a lifestyle of expressing thankfulness to God at all times. We have a million reasons for doing so. My precious mother gave me an exceptional inheritance of always being thankful.

God's Judgment on Idolatry

God's intention and longing is to manifest His presence in blessing upon the creatures He created, but if they willingly reject His rulership and choose their own way, they'll experience the hand of God in judgment (see Deuteronomy 28:15-68). Tragically, this scenario is often repeated in the Bible. When the people of God turned from Him, they inevitably turned to idolatry. This in turn provoked God to release the fire of God in judgment.

In fact, *there's a strong link in the Word of God between the fire of God and idols*. Let's look at some.

In Deuteronomy 13, God warns His people, that if anyone, without exception, ever entices them to serve other gods, they are to put that person to death. God goes on to instruct that if His people find a group of people among their own who have gone out to people of another city and sought out other idols, then all the inhabitants and livestock of that city are to be destroyed. Then all the plunder must be burned with fire so that *"none of the accursed things shall remain in your hand, that the Lord may turn from the fierceness of His anger and show you mercy"* (Deuteronomy 13:17).

God reveals His attitude again toward idolatry in Joshua 7:24-26 when Achan confessed to the sin of covetousness by taking the clothing, silver, and gold from the spoils of victory, when God had said the people were to take nothing. God called it taking *"the accursed things,"* and the punishment was being stoned and then burned with fire.

God links idolatry with covetousness in Ephesians 5:5: *"Be sure of this, that no immoral or impure man, or one who is covetous* [that is an idolater] *has any inheritance in the Kingdom of Christ and of God."* God repeats the same truth just as strongly in Colossians 3:5. In First Chronicles 14:12, when God defeated the Philistines at Baal Perazim, David instructed the people of God to burn all the enemies' idols with fire.

We must understand that God's judgments on all forms of idolatry come from His fervent love for His children, which manifests itself in a fierce jealousy over them. Exodus 34:14 says, *"You shall worship no other god, for the Lord, whose name is Jealous, is a jealous God."* Zechariah 8:2 says, *"I am zealous [or jealous] for Zion with great zeal; with great fervor I am zealous* [or jealous] *for her."*

I love that about God. I think it's wonderful that He wants my undivided devotion; that my love for Him means that much to Him. What security! What incentive to express my love to Him more ardently—the lover of my soul, the supreme love of my life.

Subtle Forms of Idolatry

You may be thinking that you can't relate to the fire of God's judgments I have listed. As we look further into the Scriptures on the subject of idolatry, we discover there are many ways in which this prevalent sin manifests itself—often very subtly.

An idol is something or someone who takes a priority place in my life to the Lord Jesus, either in my thinking, my time, my affection, my loyalty, or my obedience. What thrills us the most? What do we talk about the most? What fulfills us the most? What absorbs the majority of our thinking time? Stop and think about these questions and answers.

Most people evidence a far greater love for other pursuits than the pursuit of God. The following would be typical of many: the pursuit of sports, pleasure, and leisure-seeking, fame, food, sex, education, hobbies, lust for power, making money, more possessions, and entertainment. Every Christian would do well to take an honest look at that list, take inventory, and respond to God accordingly. That means asking God to correct us by His Spirit if any of those areas of idolatry apply to us personally, and repent before Him (see Jeremiah 14:7, 20-22).

I had to repent of spending too much time looking for bargains at garage sales and quality secondhand stores. The desire was out of all proportion and needed dealing with for what it was—a bondage. Repentance brought wonderful and permanent freedom through facing the truth.

Idolatry and the Heart

Idolatry is related to heart estrangement from God. God said to Ezekiel, when some of the elders of Israel came to ask the prophet questions, *"These men have set up their idols in their hearts, and put them before them that which causes them to stumble into iniquity.... I the Lord will answer him who comes according to the multitude of his idols that I may seize* [them] *by their heart, because they are all estranged from Me by their idols"* (Ezekiel 14:1-5). And then,

"I will set my face against that man and make him a sign and a proverb and I will cut him off from the midst of My people. Then you shall know that I am the Lord" (Ezekiel 14:8).

Idolatry is the most subtle of all sins. It lurks in the most unlikely places. I have found it is related more to the ministry God has given me, than anything else in my life. I will illustrate. It was a Friday evening at the end of an intense week of ministering daily at a spiritual leadership conference in the U.S.A. I was spending the evening and the next day in the home of the pastor and his wife who had convened the conference before flying to my next speaking assignment.

Exhausted, and relieved to have a break from the spiritual responsibilities, I crashed onto one of the sofas in their living room and said, "This is the highlight of the week for me." A little while later, I soaked in a hot bath, and as I was getting dressed again, knocked one of my little toes on an iron bed frame. Immediately I was aware of two things: (1) My toe was damaged to the extent that I couldn't walk. (2) The Holy Spirit convicted me of what I had said when I sprawled out on the sofa earlier. I had full understanding that God was not allowing me to get away with the fact that I had placed, in value, having some leisure time above the enormous privilege of being used by Him to teach His truths and lead spiritual leaders in some powerful moves of His Spirit during that week.

I repented immediately and made restitution to the pastors and one of the other speakers who was also staying in their home, all of whom had heard what I had said. I left early on Saturday evening, walking with crutches to my next plane, humbled, chastened, and grateful for the revelation of the idolatry of some leisure time, which I had all out of proportion. I was learning that the privilege of serving Jesus is higher than the price—no matter how high.

There were times when I had said, "The nearest thing to Heaven is a day at home," during the decades I spent traveling and teaching the Word of God internationally…until the day came when the Holy Spirit corrected me by reminding me that the nearest thing next to Heaven is doing the will of God, instantly, joyfully, and wholly, regardless of where I am. Again, repentance brought the forgiveness I needed.

God's mind in relation to our idolatry is vividly revealed in Jeremiah 2:11: "*Has a nation changed its gods, which are not gods? But My people have changed their Glory for what does not profit.*" And then comes a disclosure of God's heart in His reaction to the insanity of our choosing to put anything before Him. Listen to His horrified response: "'*Be astounded, O heavens, at this, and be horribly afraid; be very desolate,' says the Lord. 'For My people have committed two evils: They have forsaken **Me**, the fountain of living waters, and hewn themselves cisterns—broken cisterns that can hold no water*'" (Jeremiah 2:12-13). You notice that God didn't say His people had forsaken serving Him. They had forsaken **Him**. He had ceased to be their passion for living—their first love.

Where Is Our Priority of Focus?

I believe the most subtle of all idols is the preoccupation with our ministry responsibilities, at the expense of a delighted, devotional, intimate love relationship with the Lord. I have to guard against that all the time—especially when I'm absorbed in a big writing project, as I often am. Or, I'm searching the Scriptures and working on a new message and can get so totally immersed, that I hardly come up for air. So I'm preaching to myself. You're welcome to listen in. Be my guest. Hopefully you'll get something out of it that not only rubs off, but sticks permanently.

Perhaps you can't relate with illustrations from a Bible teacher and author. How about this one? A friend of mine told me that a fire broke out in her sewing room one day. She said that it didn't take her long to understand what God was trying to teach her. The many hours she spent in that room were deterring her from fulfilling God's priorities for her life. Repentance was the answer, which meant a change of life.

On two different occasions when counseling Christian businessmen, both of them asked me the same question: "How do I overcome the fact that every time I read the Bible before going off to work, my mind keeps wandering off onto the appointments I have for that day? I feel guilty and keep trying to concentrate, but the same patterns keep occurring."

I said to each man, "Obviously the predominant focus of your life is being successful in business, and the daily reading of the Bible is something you do because you know that's what you're supposed to do. But you're missing the purpose as to why you have a Bible. When your goal in life is to be conformed to the image of the Lord Jesus; and your priorities in life revolve around getting to know God's character and His ways, you'll discover that quality time daily in God's Word is absolutely essential to fulfill those priorities. The Lord Jesus is the Living Word."

Both men knew I had spoken the truth and were faced with making the choice of whether business pursuits were going to remain their idol, or they would repent and give God His rightful place. Their honest and sincere responses encouraged me to believe that major heart changes took place in both their lives.

God's wrath, in the Bible, is always judicial. That means the wrath of God administers justice. His judgment and wrath are part of

His awesome holiness and absolute justice. Isaiah 5:16 says, *"But the Lord of Hosts shall be exalted in judgment, and God that is holy will be sanctified in righteousness."*

A.W. Tozer says:

God's wrath is His utter intolerance of whatever degrades and destroys. Wherever the holiness of God confronts unholiness there is a conflict. God's attitude and action in the conflict are His anger. To preserve His creation, God must destroy whatever would destroy it. Every wrathful judgment of God in the history of the world has been a holy act of preservation. In His love and mercy He tells us "to flee the wrath to come."[38]

God's judgment comes because of willful sin, and sin is the most destructive force. The suffering from judgment is meant to deter us from further sin. Judgment, therefore, is an act of God's love.

God's Love Displayed in Judgment

Why do we hear so little about God's love displayed in judgment? Is it because we don't understand how these two aspects of God go together?

God can only love us as perfectly as He is holy. *"For You alone are holy"* (Revelation 15:4). God is only as just as He is holy. *"He is the Rock, His work is perfect; for all His ways are justice, a God of truth and without injustice. Righteous and upright is He"* (Deuteronomy 32:4). His judgments are a reflection of His perfect love and perfect justice.

Remove God's judgments and justice and we're left with nothing more than a celestial Santa Claus-type of a god. That image is light years away from the awesome God of the Bible, who says, *"The Lord shall judge His people. It is a fearful thing to fall into the hands of the living God"* (Hebrews 10:30-31).

When we major on God's mercy, and minor on God's judgments, we avoid taking verses like Jeremiah 5:22 seriously: *"'Do you not fear Me,' says the Lord. 'Will you not tremble at My presence?'"* We can only respect God, take Him seriously, worship and obey Him to the deepest degree that we understand every aspect of His awesome Personhood, which includes His judgments.

Paul gave a significant and profound testimony when he stated in Acts 20:26-27, *"Therefore I testify to you this day that I am innocent of the blood of all men. For I have not shunned to declare to you **the whole counsel of God.**"* In the next verse, Paul makes it clear that he was addressing spiritual leaders when he gave this powerful testimony. *"Therefore take heed to yourselves and to all the flock, among which the Holy Spirit made you overseers to shepherd the church of God"* (Acts 20:28).

As teachers of God's Word, every one of us will give an account at the Judgment Seat of Christ as to whether we avoided studying and then teaching on the judgment of God, or not. And whether it was kept in balance with His mercy and grace. Food for thought!

God's Mercy and Judgment

The fire of God's judgment along with His justice and mercy are vividly displayed in the account in Genesis 18 and 19 of Abraham's intercession, and the destruction of Sodom and Gomorrah, and in Ezekiel 16:49. The fire of God's judgment fell because of the blatant, unrepented-of sins of pride, laziness, overeating, idolatry, sexual perversion, and lack of concern for the poor and needy. Genesis 18:20 says their sins were very grave in God's sight.

God's great mercy was first of all revealed by His response to Abraham's attempts at interceding to God for Sodom and Gomorrah to be spared from annihilation. God said He would spare the cities if ten righteous persons were found. It is important to observe that

God didn't terminate His conversation with Abraham concerning his request. I believe Abraham stopped short of continuing to ask God for a display of His mercy. He asked only six times. Seven is the number of completion. We know from studying the life of Moses as an intercessor for the children of Israel that Abraham could have gone further. Moses must have had a greater revelation of the mercy of God, which produced greater boldness, persistency, and faith.

God's great mercy was also revealed to Lot and his family. Even when they were so reluctant to obey the angels' orders to flee for their safety, the Bible says the angels took hold of their hands and pulled them out of the city. It is also significant to note that Lot and his family's escape was as a direct result of the mercy of God extended to them, because of their relative Abraham's life and fervent prayers to God. (See Genesis 19:29.)

The Balance of God's Character in Revival Teaching

The more thoroughly we study the history of revivals and spiritual awakenings over the centuries, the more readily we discover that God's character was proclaimed with God's love and mercy being balanced with God's holiness and judgment. However, only God knows which particular facets of His character need emphasizing at any particular time. Anyone who has studied spiritual awakenings knows that one of the messages that was uniquely used of God to bring multitudes into His Kingdom was when Jonathan Edwards frequently preached on "Sinners in the hands of an angry God."

Now that's not the title that many of us, myself included, would choose today. In fact, it's probably the last title we would want to use. But God poured out His Spirit on the preacher, his message, and then the audiences just referred to, that produced the kind of depth of repentance that we seldom see or hear about today.

I took particular note when studying the Brownsville revival in Florida, U.S.A., that evangelist Stephen Hill's preaching, which was so mightily used of God to bring about permanent change in both Christians and non-Christians, centered around the love of God, the holiness of God, and repentance of sin. In a recent conversation with that dear man of God, he and I were mutually encouraging each other about the importance of preaching and teaching these three aspects of truth. By the way, there's a fire in Stephen Hill's eyes. To me, the explanation is simple. He has repeatedly seen aspects of the glory of God...and he's ruined for the ordinary!

In the Hebrides revival (off the coast of Scotland), which was used of God to change the culture, not just the church, the emphasis of the Rev. Duncan Campbell's preaching was the holiness of God and deep repentance of sin.

The Welsh revival and spiritual awakening was characterized by intense agony of soul as people came under the convicting power of the Holy Spirit, which manifested in wailing cries that pierced the air and finally produced repentance of sin that was life-changing. This was inevitably followed by outbursts of joyous songs of worship and praise to God that were sustained throughout that history-making season.

Charles Finney taught on the holiness of God and the desperate need for repentance of sin...because our loving God is also a God of judgment in order to be just. It was not unusual during Finney's preaching for the conviction of sin to be so deep that he would temporarily have to stop preaching because the noise of the people's brokenness before God drowned out Finney's voice.

Some of the reasons why, I believe, that kind of conviction is so rare today would be:

(1) Because there are relatively few preachers/teachers who teach the depth of God's holiness from His Word.

(2) Because relatively few teach the real meaning of repentance, and the priority place it had in Jesus' ministry. Jesus
taught His disciples to teach repentance. It was the first
message Jesus taught (see Matthew 4:17) and before He
ascended into Heaven, He commanded *"that repentance
and remission of sins should be preached in His name to all
nations"* (Luke 24:47). Peter preached it in the revival
recorded in Acts 2:38 and the apostles continued to preach
it.

(3) Because the judgment of God is rarely taught.

(4) Because so little faith-filled intercession goes up before the
Lord for depth of conviction to take place.

(5) When the love of God is taught, so few times is it coupled
with the truth that *"The goodness of God leads you to
repentance"* (Romans 2:4).

Importance of Manifesting the Fruits of the Spirit

We know from First Corinthians 13:1-3 that the love of God, in
and through us, is a priority, but we're seldom taught that we're only as
loving as we are humble. The deepest repentance needed is always in
relation to pride—always! Pride is our greatest enemy, not the devil.

God's Word clearly states that the Day of the Lord is coming
when we least expect it, when *"the heavens will pass away with a
great noise, and the elements will melt with fervent heat; both the earth
and the works that are in it will be burned up"* (2 Peter 3:10). God
wants us to so believe in these pre-determined historic facts that it will
motivate us to live holy lives in readiness for the time when we will live
and reign with Him in His new Kingdom, where there is a new Heaven
and a new earth where righteousness reigns. What a prospect!

The apostle Peter goes on to say, in verse 14, that when we live
our lives with this great anticipation, it should cause us to make sure
we have no unrepented sin, and that our lives are manifesting the peace

of God. If we're always talking about the stress we're under and the negative effect it has upon us, we're obviously not experiencing God's peace. That means we need to repent of not receiving God's promised grace in our circumstances. Remember, He gives it to the humble! (See James 4:6.)

God's grace and peace are inevitably and significantly linked together in God's Word. When Paul and Peter and John greeted the believers by letters of exhortation, they said, as a way of life, *"May grace be unto you and peace from God the Father."* [These words are frequently quoted in the Epistles.] My understanding of God's grace is that it is the supernatural ability to cope in difficult circumstances, with praise on our lips, thankful hearts, and peace of mind. We either have it, or we don't.

The nearer we get to the day *"when the Lord Jesus is revealed from Heaven with His mighty angels in flaming fire taking vengeance on those who do not know God and on those who do not obey the gospel of our Lord Jesus Christ"* (2 Peter 3:7-8), the more we need to be vigilant about fulfilling God's conditions to be manifesting the fruit of the Holy Spirit, called peace, regardless of the circumstances. It's one of the strongest evidences of the life of the Lord Jesus in us, to non-believers. Satan cannot fake it.

Paul tells us in verse 12 of Second Thessalonians 3, that the reason for everything he's been writing to the Thessalonian believers about is, *"that the name of the Lord Jesus Christ may be glorified in you and you in Him."* And then he explains to them and us, how that will take place: *"according to the grace of our God and the Lord Jesus Christ"* (2 Thessalonians 3:12).

God's Righteous Judgments

In Isaiah 66, God gives us some understanding of His ways in judgment, rewarding those who adhere to His priorities and equally punishing those who don't. In verse 2, after speaking of His unparalleled greatness, God describes the person who impresses Him: "*But on this one will I look* [gets His attention]; *on him who is poor* [knows he has a need] *and a contrite spirit* [one who lives a life of repentance of sin] *and who trembles at My Word* [has the fear of the Lord upon him, takes Him seriously and obeys Him at any cost]."

In contrast, in Isaiah 66, verses 3 and 4, God describes those who live according to their own rules and disregard God's instructions and terms, and consequently come under His righteous judgments: "*So I will choose their delusions, and bring their fears on them; because when I called, no one answered, when I spoke they did not hear; but they did evil before My eyes, and chose that in which I do not delight*" (Isaiah 66:4). In verses 5 and 6, God encourages all those who have been misjudged by others in the Body of Christ for obedience to Him, that He will vindicate them in His time. That's also part of His righteous judgments. Praise His wonderful Name!

In Isaiah 66:7-13, God describes to us the process of allowing the Holy Spirit to conceive a burden for revival praying in us, and the cost of bearing the burden, and travailing until God answers. "*For as soon as Zion* [the people of God] *was in labor, she gave birth to her children*" (Isaiah 66:8). He also explains that as a God of justice and righteous judgment, there will always be fulfillment, never a still-birth. How faithful He is! "*'Shall I bring to the time of birth, and not cause delivery?' Says the Lord*" (Isaiah 66:9).

Then in verses 14-17, God explains His righteous judgments on those who rebel against His revealed plan for their salvation. That is where God separates the tares from the wheat. "*The hand of the Lord shall be known to His servants. And His indignation to His enemies*" (Isaiah 66:14).

God does it by demonstrating that He's the God who answers by fire. "*For behold the Lord will come with fire and with His chariots like a whirlwind, to render His anger and fury, and His rebuke with flames of fire. For by fire and by His sword the Lord will judge all flesh; and the slain of the Lord shall be many"* (Isaiah 66:15-16).

God's Eternal Judgments Are Completely Righteous

We find that the righteousness of God's judgments are spelled out with stark reality and clarity in the Book of Revelation. In Revelation 14:6, we read that there will be an *"angel in the midst of Heaven having the everlasting gospel to preach to those who dwell on the earth—to every nation, tribe, tongue and people—saying with a loud voice, 'Fear God and give glory to Him, for the hour of **His judgment** has come; and worship Him who made Heaven and earth, the sea and springs of water."* That means, everyone will have the chance in God's economy to submit to Him and His plan of salvation and to be spared eternal judgment. This truth is promised again in Matthew 24:14: *"And this gospel of the Kingdom will be preached in all the world as a witness to all nations, and then the end will come."*

In Revelation 4:9, another angel is written about who just as clearly announces with a loud voice that:

If anyone worships the beast and his image and receives the mark on his forehead or on his hand, he himself shall also drink of the wine of the wrath of God, which is poured out full strength into the cup of His indignation. He shall be tormented with fire and brimstone in the presence of the holy angels and in the presence of the Lamb. And the smoke of their torment ascends forever and ever; and they have no rest day or night who worship the beast and his image, and whoever receives the mark of his name.

I have purposely spelled out every word of that horrendous warning, because it is truth. And because I can't bear to think that anyone would read this book and not have the opportunity to know what the opportunities and options are. One is to choose submission to Jesus Christ, God's Son, and His plan of salvation. The only other option is to reject Christ's offer of eternal life by not receiving the Lord Jesus Christ by faith as your Savior and Redeemer and not making Him Lord of your life, and then suffer the consequences that are described above.

We either choose Christ's plan for our lives, which produces eternal life, or we choose satan's plan, which will produce everlasting separation from God, and be subject to His judgments. We do ourselves the ultimate favor by choosing Christ, the only One who said, *"I am the way, the truth and the life"* (John 14:6).

In Revelation 14:18 we read about an angel who was given power over fire, and again in Revelation chapter 15, we see that fire is an integral part of God's judgments. This time they are described in very unusual imagery. John saw:

> **Something like a sea of glass mingled with fire**, and *those who have the victory over the beast, over his image and over his mark and over the number of his name,* **standing on the sea of glass**, *having harps of God. And they sing…"Great and marvelous are Your works, Lord God Almighty! Just and true are Your ways, O King of the saints! Who shall not fear You, O Lord, and glorify Your name? For You alone are holy. For all nations shall come and worship before You. For **your judgments** have been manifested"* (Revelation 15:2-4).

If that isn't dramatic enough, what follows in chapter 16 is an increase of an utterly awesome display of God's wrath, glory, and power as seven angels dispense God's judgments upon the earth.

The first angel poured out his bowl of the wrath of God and loathsome sores came upon those who had rejected God's offer of His Son. The second angel's action caused the sea to become blood and every living thing in the sea died. Then, after the third angel poured out his bowl on the rivers and springs of water and they became blood, the angel declared the righteous judgments of God. He said, *"You are righteous, O Lord, the One who is and who was and who is to be, because You have judged these things. For they have shed the blood of saints and prophets, and You have given them blood to drink. For it is their just due"* (Revelation 16:5-6).

Here again, God is reiterating the truth that the law of sowing and reaping is inevitable. In verse 7, another angel affirms the justice of God by saying, *"Even so, Lord God Almighty, true and righteous are Your judgments"* (Revelation 16:7).

So deep is man's blatant rebellion against God's rulership of his life, that even when the fourth angel was given the power to cause the sun to scorch men with great heat, the Bible says, *"and they blasphemed the name of God who had power over these plagues; and they did not repent and give Him glory"* (Revelation 16:9).

Again when the fifth angel caused pain to come upon people so that they gnawed their tongues because of its intensity, the Bible says they still blasphemed God and did not repent of their deeds. Then, when the greatest earthquake took place that has ever occurred since men were on the earth, which causes the islands and mountains to disappear, and enormous weights of hail rained down from Heaven, in verse 21 we're told that man's reaction was still to blaspheme God, rather than repent of their sin. Are you, dear reader, beginning to more clearly understand the righteous fire of God in judgment?

One of the most awesome and breathtaking descriptions of our magnificent Master, the Lord Jesus, in the fire of His judgments is found in Revelation 19:11-16:

> *Now I saw heaven opened, and behold a white horse. And He who sat on Him was called Faithful and True, and in righteousness He judges and makes war. His eyes were like flames of fire, and on His head were many crowns. He had a name written that no one knew except Himself. He was clothed with a robe dipped in blood, and His name is called The Word of God. And the armies in heaven, clothed in fine*

*linen, white and clean, followed Him on white horses. Now
out of His mouth goes a sharp sword, that with it He should
strike the nations. And He himself will rule them with a rod
of iron. He himself treads the winepress of the fierceness
and wrath of Almighty God. And He has on His robe and on
His thigh a name written: KING OF KINGS AND LORD
OF LORDS.*

Now that's a stunning description of the ruling, reigning Monarch
of the universe in His supreme authority and magnificent splendor,
with an aura of mystique, *"He had a name written that no one knew
except Himself"* (verse 12) along with His known names, King of
Kings and Lord of Lords. That is the One before whom I find myself
trembling and standing in speechless awe and breathtaking silent worship.

This is the One, in His absolute justice and righteous judgment,
who ultimately captures the beast and the false prophet and casts them
alive into the lake of fire burning with brimstone. And then He kills the
kings of the earth and their armies who came to make war against
Him, with the sword that proceeded from His mouth. That's the lion of
the tribe of Judah roaring with divine authority and executing it with
God power.

For a thousand years satan will be chained and cast into the bot-
tomless pit which will be sealed (see Revelation 20:2). Then he will be
released for a time and will deceive the nations and gather them to war
against God's people. But the fire of God's judgment will then come
down from God, out of heaven and devour them (see Revelation 20:7-
9).

Finally, the liar, the deceiver, the destroyer, the accuser, the
divider, the tempter—satan himself, the ultimate rebel—will be cast
into the lake of fire and brimstone where the beast and the false
prophet are. And they will be tormented day and night forever and
ever. That's total justice and righteous judgment.

How dare any creatures of the dust have the audacity to think they can oppose the One who had the first word in creating the universe— the One who upholds it by the word of His power. The One who will have every other word needed to cause every person in it to ultimately bow their knees and open their mouths to acknowledge that Jesus Christ is Lord to the glory of God! Again, I tremble before His magnificent, matchless, majestic presence in awestruck silent worship.

At the great white throne of judgment, the Bible gives us a description of what I consider to be the ultimate display of God's awesome power. In Revelation 20:11 we read that John saw a preview of this historic event. He said, *"I saw a great white throne and Him who sat on it, from whose face the earth and heaven fled away. And there was no place for them."*

Please think with me about what you've just read. This mind-boggling Being is so indescribably powerful that He doesn't have to blink an eyelid, speak a word, or move a muscle. He is so transcendingly awesome, other-worldly, nothing-to-be-compared-with, in spacey power, that the heavens and earth disappear when ***His face shows up!!***

The ultimate righteous judge of all the universe took His place and judged all the dead from the land and the sea by what had been recorded in the books about each one's works (see Revelation 20:13). *"Then death and Hades were cast into the lake of fire....And anyone not found written in the Book of Life was cast into the lake of fire"* (Revelation 20:14-15).

Because the heaven and earth and sea disappeared, God created new ones (see Revelation 21:1) to contain *"the holy city, New Jerusalem which comes down out of Heaven from God, prepared as a bride adorned for her husband"* (Revelation 21:2).

Then we read the ultimate comfort statement of all time for those who have made Jesus Christ the Lord of their lives and experienced suffering. *"And God will wipe away every tear from their eyes; there shall be no more death nor sorrow nor crying. There shall be no more pain, for the former things have passed away"* (Revelation 21:4). WOW! WOW! WOW! WOW! What an all-conquering, undefeated, victorious champion Jesus is! What else can we do but adore and worship Him, and then instantly, wholly, and joyfully obey Him as a way of life?

SECTION SEVEN

THE FIRE OF GOD
IN PERSECUTION AND SUFFERING

I n His faithfulness to His disciples when on earth, the Lord Jesus warned them and all future disciples that persecution in some form is part of the price of following Him wholeheartedly.

> *"If the world hates you, you know that it hated Me before it hated you.... A servant is not greater than his master. If they persecuted Me, they will also persecute you.... But that the word might be fulfilled which was written in their law, 'They hated Me without a cause'"* (John 15:18,20,25).

So why are we always amazed when we hear of either the collective or individual fires of persecution being ignited among Jesus' dedicated disciples? After all, it's simply the fulfillment of prophetic statements. And every seriously committed servant of our Heavenly Commander-in-Chief should face the reality and possibility of having the unique honor of suffering for the sake of the gospel.

When the early apostles were imprisoned overnight, released by an angel, and found themselves on trial again before the Jewish hierarchy, their response to repeated commands not to teach any more in

Jesus' name was, *"We ought to obey God rather than men"* (Acts 5:29). And they proceeded to do so. This resulted in the apostles being severely beaten.

With Jesus' words still ringing in their ears, their magnificent response to this injustice and pain was, *"So they departed from the presence of the council, rejoicing that they were counted worthy to suffer shame for His name. And daily in the temple and in every home, they did not cease teaching and preaching Jesus as the Christ"* (Acts 5:41-42). The same fires of persecution still burn fiercely today in many parts of the world. And God's people are responding with the same kind of Christlike love.

The Fire of God's Love

Our son-in-law, John Bills, who we call J.B. because our son's name is also John, is a leader and teacher in Youth With A Mission. J.B. has a heart for suffering humanity. He has been on several missionary journeys to a communist-controlled country to encourage and help provide for the needs of the pastors and believers where they are frequently persecuted for their commitment to Christ. The pastors have many times been imprisoned and mistreated under horrible conditions. One of those young pastors, who we will call David for security reasons, was imprisoned and severely beaten before being put in a cell with 14 other people who were there for committing various crimes. None of them were Christians.

It wasn't long before David had witnessed to them about the reality of the Lord Jesus and led them all to Christ. It became obvious to the guards that these prisoners had become Christians, so they decided to stop David from witnessing by putting him in solitary confinement. High up on the wall of each cell was a small grated window, which faced out into the corridor. Each day, David would pray out loud, sing worship and praise songs to the Lord, and quote as many Scriptures as he could remember because the guards had taken his Bible and destroyed it when they incarcerated him. There were other prisoners in solitary confinement who could hear him, and they would call out, asking him with whom he was talking? This resulted in David loudly explaining the way of salvation, and several more prisoners committed their lives to Christ.

Then one day, this brave pastor heard a faint sound of a woman's voice. The more intently he listened he realized that the voice was coming from a small hole on the floor level in the corner of his cell. Because there were no toilets in the cells, and David's cell was at the end of the corridor, all the human excrement ran through the small holes from the other cells into his cell. The only way he could hear what the young woman was asking him, which were questions about his faith in Christ, and for him to reply, was to get down on his hands and knees and put his face down on the sewage to speak to her. In this way she heard the way of salvation and was converted to Christ.

Pastor David had been converted while he was in a refugee camp in Thailand, during the 80s, where Youth With A Mission workers had explained to him the way of salvation, and over many months had discipled him. He was then in his late twenties. At the time of this story he was now in his early thirties and without his Bible. But each day he asked God to bring back to his remembrance the wonderful Bible teaching he had learned from the Y.W.A.M. missionaries.

God answered those prayers, and through those shocking circumstances David was able to daily disciple that new convert over many weeks. Finally they were released from prison. That young Asian pastor and evangelist is a first-class hero of my son-in-law and daughter and my husband Jim and mine. His life constantly inspires and challenges us all. He and others have suffered many subsequent imprisonments, but Jesus' promise in Matthew 16:18 is being powerfully fulfilled in that country: *"I will build My church and the gates of hell will not prevail against it."*

The fires of persecution are no match for the fire of God's love when a servant of Christ has asked to be consumed by it with the Holy Spirit's flame, *"The love of God has been poured out in our hearts by the Holy Spirit who was given to us"* (Romans 5:5).

Dr. A.B. Simpson, a profound Bible teacher, once wrote, "The Holy Spirit kindles in the soul the fires of love, the flame that melts our selfishness, and pours out our being in tenderness, sacrifice and service. And the same fire of love is the fusing, uniting flame which makes Christians one, even as the volcanic tide that rolls down the mountain fuses into one current everything in its course."[39]

In one of the apostle Paul's letters to Timothy, he makes a statement that we all need to understand about the inevitability of persecution to those who are willing to make Christlikeness their ultimate goal: *"Yes, and all who desire to live godly in Christ Jesus will suffer persecution"* (2 Timothy 3:12). Sadly, many times that prediction is realized through others in the Body of Christ. The sure cure is to do what Jesus told us to do. He said we are to love, bless, and pray for those who persecute us. Jesus is undoubtedly the ultimate authority on that subject, and when we choose to obey Him, we discover we've tapped into the miraculous. Jesus, the donor, gives us a heart transplant that heals and frees us from pain. And it doesn't cost us a penny. Our part is to ask for it, submit to the person of the Holy Spirit, believe that He is working in us, and obey whatever He tells us to do. He will give us opportunities in His way and time to demonstrate His love through us.

Because the Bible says. *"Love never fails,"* our Christ-like response to those who have wronged us not only changes us but is often the very thing that changes them. Some of the greatest miracles I have personally witnessed and experienced have been through living what I have just written, because God's love is the most powerful force in the universe. It's irresistible, irreplaceable, immeasurable, unstoppable, and combustible. It can explode in the midst of the fires of persecution, as illustrated in the following story.

The fire of resentments can ravage us, or we can submit to the fire of God to burn them out. We're either left charred through bitterness or changed by the fire of God's holy flame to have Christ's heart toward those who have wronged us.

Santosh was an uneducated farmer of an outcast branch of society, living in a village in Maharashtra, India, who became a devout follower of the Lord Jesus Christ. A missionary was present at his baptism service who invited Santosh and his family to go to a city mission, where they could learn to read and write, study the Bible, and get better acquainted with the Lord and His people.

Santosh agreed to go, provided he could find someone to look after his field and home while they were away. He owned a piece of land where he grew crops to support his family, along with a few odd jobs of work. However, one night when he was coming home late from the market, he found that all his crops had been set on fire. It was harvesttime and he was preparing to start cutting the crops the following week. He watched as his next year's supply of food went up in flames.

It was because he had become a Christian. Santosh's relatives and neighbors had already beaten him and pulled the tiles off the roof of his house. His wife had to suffer taunts and insults from the other women and they falsely accused her of having an adulterous relationship with another man. His children had mud and filth thrown at them. His young daughter, Shanta, was nearly crushed by a bullock cart while she was playing on the road. The driver purposely drove faster to run over her, but God intervened and someone saw her in time and rescued her.

Through all this persecution, this humble servant of the Lord was able to receive God's grace and the accompanying peace of God filled his mind. He was able to appropriate God's love, by faith, for his enemies as the Lord had told him to do in His Word. But, when this Christian farmer saw his family's year's supply of food being destroyed before his eyes, a terrible fear and resentment gripped his heart and he wondered what he would do. He looked to God for help.

Then he remembered that in God's Word it says that all our works will be tried by fire at the Judgment Seat of Christ. And the fire of God's Spirit began to burn in his heart. Questions seared their way into his thoughts. Had Santosh really given God everything, all that he was and had, all his possessions? Was he really abandoned to God, to love and live for Him for Himself alone? Was God sufficient, was He all? Santosh replied, "Yes, Lord, You can take anything…anything and everything." Then it happened.

The fire of God's Spirit burned to ashes every ounce of bitterness toward those who had persecuted him, and then filled this lowly, outcast Indian believer with the fire of God's love. As a bonus blessing, the joy of the Lord overflowed from this heart set free. He raised his hands and found himself praising God profusely in words he had never known before.

Santosh explained that he had previously been baptized in water, but now he knew what it meant to be baptized with the Holy Spirit and fire. Because of God's flawless character, He provided for Santosh's family in other ways. They went to the city, were taught to read and write, studied God's Word, and were better equipped to be a powerful witness in their village upon returning. God was completely faithful to meet all their needs in His way and time.[40]

God's Sovereignty

I am going to take this opportunity, for the first time in print, to give the following personal testimony. My conviction is there are times when God initially fills us with His Spirit and He graces us with another language to express our praises to Him. And there are other times that He chooses not to, for His sovereign purposes. A surrendered will doesn't dictate the terms. I had been unquestionably filled with the Holy Spirit, with a totally changed life to validate it, including several of the other gifts of the Spirit operating freely to bless others, for a full six years before God released to me the gift of tongues. And I never had the slightest fear, reserve or unbelief about doing so at any time, in case some readers may presume that any one of the above was the reason why it didn't happen before.

For me, the infilling of the Holy Spirit produced a whole new passionate desire to know God intimately, plus an insatiable hunger for His Word, a marked increase in power to witness, and to pray more effectively for others. I wasn't short-changed!

Six years later, God came upon me quietly when alone with Him in prayer and gave me another prayer language. Apart from having another dimension of praising the Lord, I have found a great benefit has been to use the gift when interceding for others. In fact, the Holy Spirit has given me numerous different languages over the intervening years to be used for that powerful purpose.

My understanding is that the Holy Spirit decides that it is more productive for His purposes that I, or others with whom I may be praying, are not cognitive of what He is saying to the Father on behalf of others. If satanic forces are around, they don't get in on the secrets either. All I know is that God's hand is moved in powerful ways to meet the needs of the recipients when I obey the promptings of the Holy Spirit to intercede in that way. It is not an automatic thing with me, otherwise it would cancel out my need to be waiting on God for specific directions in intercession, which produces the ultimate effectiveness. In my book, *Intercession, Thrilling and Fulfilling,* I address that important subject in chapter 15.

There was a time in Youth With A Mission when a certain leader was going through a very difficult time in his marriage. Every few months he would report on this situation that had arisen and he was at a loss to know what to do. A few of us had been dealing with this situation for some time without the needed breakthrough.

At a time when I was overseas, speaking at spiritual leadership conferences, teamed with other international Bible teachers, an urgent phone call came through to Loren Cunningham and myself, concerning a serious crisis that had arisen related to the above circumstances. We were desperate, and knew that desperate prayer was the only course of action. Having made sure our hearts were clean before God, and inviting the Holy Spirit to take complete control, we took authority over the powers of darkness in Jesus' name and silenced them, should they be around. We then expressed our faith and trust in God to work mightily through us as we waited on Him for His directions, presuming nothing.

After a time of silence, to my amazement and somewhat to my embarrassment, in obedience to the promptings of the Holy Spirit, I started to speak clearly in the strangest language I had ever heard in my life. (And I have heard numerous ones.) I continued to do so until prompted to stop. I was kneeling beside a chair which faced into a wall on the opposite side of the room from where Loren was kneeling. He was kneeling before a sofa and had his head buried into it with his back to me, so I never heard a word that he uttered. When I commented to Loren about the strangeness of my unknown intercessory prayer language, he announced that he had been given precisely the same language at the same time. He could hear me but I couldn't hear him. We both marveled at the synchronization of the Holy Spirit's workings and worshiped God. We sensed that the Holy Spirit had conversed with the Father through us on behalf of that needy couple in some profound and completely confidential way, and that God had answered.

Within a week, we were informed that there was a major breakthrough in the lives of those precious missionaries, which has remained to my knowledge to this day. God's thoughts and ways are higher than ours, in fact Psalm 18: 30 says they are perfect. You can't improve on perfection.

The Overcoming Love of God

Satan can counterfeit a number of the things of the Spirit, but neither he nor his demons can counterfeit the love of God, which is based in humility. Satanic forces are full of pride and therefore don't even understand this quality of love, let alone know how to operate in it. Humility outsmarts them every time.

The following story illustrates how a high caste Brahmin Hindu priest was confronted with the revelation of God's love. This man was a trainer of Hindu priests. He learned the Hindu scriptures thoroughly and could quote many texts from memory, including Gita 4:7-8 which reads. "I, Krisna come to seek and destroy the sinner." Then, one day he was in his library reading through a resource book, the New Testament. He came across the verse in Luke 19:10 (NIV): *"For the Son of Man came to seek and to save what was lost."* He read on.

Impressed by the compassionate character of the God of the Bible, this Hindu gave his life to Christ. It was 1962. Kicked out of his home, he found himself in prison two years later. Every two hours he was beaten by the police. He had no food for four days and nights. His leg was broken as he was kicked in the beatings. And this was but the beginning. He was severely persecuted for his faith, being twenty two times held in police custody, thrown in jail three times, and spent a total of two years in jail. Yet he persevered.

This man was consumed with love for God and God's love for his people in a nation where persecution of Christians is rampant. The fire of God's love produced deep spiritual ambition in his heart and courageous boldness to declare, "We have paid the price for our nation, now the nation rightfully belongs to the Lord and to His people." I'm sure there was a thunderous "**Amen**" in Heaven when that statement was made.

Jesus' Warnings and Encouragements

The Church of Jesus Christ is suffering great persecution in many nations today; perhaps more than ever in history. And my conviction is that it will increase. The nearer we get to the coming again of the Lord Jesus, the greater we'll experience the polarization of light and darkness. The outpouring of the Holy Spirit in revival on God's people and spiritual awakening upon the lost, and the unleashing of satanic forces in fury, vileness and violence will both be magnified. There will be no place for mediocrity. The fire of God will get hotter and more intense in displaying His glory, and the forces of darkness will spew out their vicious venom in revolt to it.

But ultimately they are nothing more than fallen angels doomed to eternal destruction. And I'm not impressed with that status. The head of our army is the ruling, reigning Monarch of the universe who had the first word in relation to this universe and will have the last. One man plus God is always a majority regardless of the numerical strengths of the opposition.

When Peter was imprisoned for preaching about the Lord Jesus, the early disciples had an all night prayer meeting for his release. God answered by sending an angel while the guards were sleeping to give Peter a personal escort out of the prison while supernaturally opening the locked doors en route. How's that for deluxe service. You can't beat it.

But then again, as we look into the Word of God we find that Jesus predicted special treatment for those persecuted for His sake. He clearly stated in His Sermon on the Mount, when teaching the Beatitudes, that God's blessing would be upon *"those who are persecuted for righteousness' sake, for theirs is the Kingdom of Heaven."* And if it included being reviled against, and all kinds of evil and false accusations being said against us, we're not only blessed by God, but we're to get really excited about the rewards God is stockpiling up on our account (see Matthew 5:10-12).

Because the Lord Jesus is a magnificent Master, we not only discover that obeying Him pays great dividends, but His retirement plan is *out of this world!*

To get the balanced God-view on persecution, and to understand His justice, we need to remind ourselves what Jesus promised when He told us to go into all the world and preach the gospel. He said that everything we give up in order to be obedient to that mandate, He would give us one hundredfold more in return. Wow! That means that in time, when He sees we have passed many tests, we're truly living for His glory, and being obedient to His priorities, He will actually embarrass us with His blessings. What a deal! But there are two more words added to the contract: "with persecutions" (Mark 10:9,30).

Immediately after the above discourse with His disciples, Jesus told them that He was going to have to suffer greatly before being resurrected from the dead. But they didn't get it. Suffering is an inevitable part of the discipleship course, if we're really going to follow Jesus and submit to the dealings of the Holy Spirit to conform us into Christ's image.

Listen to another one of Jesus' warnings and encouragements. *"In Me you may have peace. In the world you will have tribulation, but be of good cheer, I have overcome the world"* (John 16:33). My paraphrase of that verse is "inevitably you will experience suffering, but don't get up-tight and fearful, because I am in control and I am bigger than anything that can come against you."

God Is In Control

I don't know a more amazing story to illustrate this teaching of Jesus than what happened to a teenage girl during the terrorist attack on the World Trade Center in New York, on September 11, 2001, when the Twin Towers were demolished. She was praying for help while making her way down the stairs of the building along with many others who were trying to escape the inferno, when suddenly everything around her collapsed. She found herself in pitch darkness, alone, standing upright, with her body wedged between steel beams and fallen debris. She couldn't move. But she was alive, and so she prayed, asking God to do something to miraculously deliver her.

The way God answered that young girl's prayer staggers my imagination and leaves me once again in total awe of our mind-boggling God. He simply put her to sleep! And 24 hours later she woke up, hearing the sounds of rescuers digging their way through the rubble, looking for any survivors. In due time they discovered her, and were amazed at her unexplainable—to-them, condition.

Having just had a long sleep while being propped up on all sides, she came out in good shape, testifying that God had obviously answered her simple prayer of faith. My jaw fell open and my eyes were nearly "out like organ stops" on the two occasions I saw and heard that girl tell her story on the CNN network.

That reminds me of what the prophet Isaiah tells us in Isaiah 26:3 about having perfect peace when we focus our minds fully on Jesus, and trust in His character, no matter what! You can't have more peace of mind than having the (God-given) ability to have an extended time of sleep under such horrific circumstances as that teenager experienced. An atheist would have a hard time trying to convince her there is no God! My guess is, he wouldn't have the nerve to try.

Our Response to the Persecuted Church

We need to have a realistic understanding about where the Church stands today in relation to worldwide persecution, so that we can make the appropriate responses. Reliable missiologists and research experts tell us there have been more people martyred for their faith in Jesus Christ in the 20th and 21st centuries than in all previous centuries combined. We're talking about 100 million martyrs, according to *World Missions Digest*. In the very places where there have been the greatest number of people coming to Christ, the accompanying persecution has been accelerated; such as in Latin America, sub-Sahara Africa and Asia. Those of us who still live in places where there is religious freedom have an enormous responsibility and privilege to be involved in helping to alleviate the burdens of those who are persecuted for their faith. Believe me, at the judgment seat of Christ we will have to give an account of what we did or didn't do for them.

God's Word makes it very clear as to what we as believers should be doing right now in relation to the persecuted Church worldwide. For those who are in prison we are instructed to pray for them: *"Remember those in prison as if you were their fellow prisoners, and those who are mistreated as if you yourselves were suffering"* (Hebrews 13:3).

When the persecuted Christians globally are asked how best the rest of the Body of Christ worldwide can help them, their immediate response is always the same, "Please pray for us." They are acutely aware that they need the miraculous grace of God to cope in their difficult circumstances more than anything else:

- The grace and faith to remain strong in their trust in God when they cannot trace Him.
- The grace to endure the long separations from loved ones through imprisonment.
- The faith to believe for the miraculous provisions of needs when they are so often deprived of the normal means of meeting those needs…to name just a few.

I was deeply touched when I read the following account in the October-December issue of *Strategic Times Journal*, published by Issachar Frontier Mission Strategies:

Dr. Miriam Adeney, Associate Professor of Religion at Seattle Pacific University, was invited to speak at the Moscow Congress because her work in women's studies has been useful to the Soviet Christian women. She reports: "In my own teaching, after I told stories about strong Christian women around the world, I invited the participants to do the same. 'Would you tell us about some of the strong women who have encouraged you?'" People were eager to tell their stories, and one after the other they did so. A shy, fortyish woman was one of the volunteers. "I'd like to tell you about a strong woman who is a model to me," she said in a soft voice. "This woman's husband was sent into exile for his faith. They had eight children. Then the woman was herself arrested and brought before the interrogation committee. She carried her baby daughter with her.

'Either renounce your faith in God, or we will see that your children are killed,' the interrogators told her. For some time she couldn't say anything. Finally she said, 'I have to rely on God to protect my children.' She laid her infant daughter on the bench, and walked out the door and into prison. One year later, she was so sick that the prison doctor refused to allow the prison authorities to interrogate her anymore, and she was released. When she returned home, the baby daughter who had been left on the bench came running to meet her. She found that all her children were alive. Eventually her husband came back from exile, and they had a ninth child. That woman lived to be ninety. All her children grew up healthy and in the Lord."

Then the shy woman added, "I was the baby who was left on the bench. She was my mother."

To be present with these people who had proved faithful at great cost was sobering, humbling, and energizing.[41]

There's a very solemn warning to us who live in freedom from persecution related to those who do not, with many deprivations. *"He who closes his ear to the cry of the poor, will himself cry out and not be heard"* (Proverbs 21:13). Simply put, it means our cries to God for help in times of need will go unheeded if we don't heed the cries of the needy for help when it's within our power to do so.

Listen to the judgment of God that comes upon those who have no involvement in helping the poor and needy. *"For wicked men are found among My people...they have become great and rich, they have grown sleek and fat. They know no bounds in deeds of wickedness, they judge not with justice the cause of the fatherless, to make it prosper and they do not defend the rights of the needy. Shall I not punish them for these things? Says the Lord and shall I not avenge Myself on a nation such as this?"* (Jeremiah 5:26-29)

For decades, my husband Jim and I have interceded regularly and fervently for our persecuted brothers and sisters internationally. But in recent years that responsibility has become much more fulfilling as we are now able to receive Brother Andrew's Open Doors printed materials. What a wealth of specific up-to-date information we are able to use as prayer fuel. Without releasing their real names at times, for security reasons, Open Doors literature gives the information on individuals and groups in specific countries and their stressful circumstances. The mailing address in the U.S.A. is: Open Doors, P.O. Box 27001, Santa Ana, CA 92799.

Just recently, those on the mailing list were able to rejoice over answered prayer for an innocent Christian man from Lima, Peru who was unjustly imprisoned for over eight years. He used it as an opportunity to share the gospel with many other prisoners and became a pastor to them. He shared that the letters he received from Christians in many nations who had been informed of his circumstances through the Open Doors newsletters, and who encouraged him to believe that God would answer their prayers for his release, brought tremendous joy and were like oxygen to him during those long years.

Through this wonderful ministry to the global suffering Church, we are also able to send money to Open doors, as they distribute Bibles and leadership training materials, as well as much needed materials for children in the lands where Christians have no other means of obtaining them.

One Christian woman for whom prayer is requested is in a predominantly Muslim country, married to a Muslim. She has two children and she lives with the horrible situation where the government is trying to take her children away from her so that they won't be raised as Christians. Imagine the stress. There's another young girl from a Muslim home who has been converted to Christ. He appeared three times to her in dreams, so she secretly asked Christians to tell her more about Jesus, resulting in her conversion. She knows that if her father found out that she had become a Christian he would most likely kill her.

I give these examples in the hope that you, dear reader, will be motivated to regularly engage in intercession for the many precious believers who are asking us to remember them, and give of our resources as the Holy Spirit directs. Let us pray that their faith would not fail and that God will supernaturally sustain them, and by His grace miraculously provide for them.

The Fellowship of Christ's Sufferings

When we examine Paul's impassioned prayer to know God in intimate friendship as in Philippians 3:10, we discover that it covers the depth of the spectrum needed to realize the fulfillment of the request. *"O that I may know Him and the power of His resurrection,* (the fire of enduement for service) *and may share in the fellowship of His sufferings,* (multi-faceted sufferings) *becoming like Him in His death."* So many of God's servants want to know Him and experience His resurrection power, but have very little understanding of what it means to experientially enter into the fellowship of Christ's sufferings and to die to self's rights and become conformed to Christ's image.

Many years ago when I first prayed Philippians 3:10, I knew that in order to share with Christ's sufferings I would have to suffer. That was simple and logical. Because of God's unfathomable love and infinite wisdom, I also knew that I could trust Him as to how and when it all worked out. By far the greatest preparation for entering into the fellowship of Christ's sufferings, is to study

God's character, facet by facet from His Word. The revelation of God's character and His ways from His Word are unquestionably the greatest anchors to keep our faith strong and secure against the howling gales of perplexity, pain, and unanswered prayers.

In February 1993, I woke one night around 2:30 A.M. with lower back pain. I immediately prayed the following prayer. "Dear Lord, bring the maximum glory to Your name through my having this pain. Show me whatever it is You're trying to teach me. Please reveal to me the causes and/or the purposes related to this situation. Please give me any directions I am to take in relation to it. Thank you that You will answer these prayers in Your own way and time."

Waiting for God's answers to my questions, I totally relinquished all my rights to be healed, and left the outcome with Him. After four months of silence, God broke through by answering me from the book of Job, that I was in a severe testing time and that He was in complete control. I reiterated to God again that I only wanted that He be glorified to the maximum through this affliction.

One year after the initial pain, in obedience to much prayer and God's direction, I had major back surgery. I came out of it with increased pain and a severely damaged nervous system. For the next two years I was unable to go to church, travel or speak at meetings, or continue writing my book on intercession, which I had started. All I could do was to lie on my left side, worship and praise God, read my Bible, and intercede for others—which I did a lot. Going anywhere in a car aggravated my pain even when lying down in the back seat on a foam mattress pad. So I was grounded. My identity was not, and is not, in being an international Bible teacher and author, but being in intimate friendship with God. So the enormous change in my circumstances did not produce an identity crisis. Prior to this time in my life I always had compassion for suffering people. But now I have identification—a vast difference.

It also gave me a tremendous appreciation for the multitudes of my fellow Christians worldwide who were cut off from being able to have fellowship with other believers. Not to be able to attend a church service for two years was particularly hard. It was a time of loneliness that I had never anticipated or known anything about. We have no idea how much we need each other in the Body of Christ until we're cut off from having the rich privilege of Christian fellowship.

My beloved husband chose to stay by my side all the time, other than when going to a few church services. Only God can reward him for what he sacrificed without complaint. And our precious daughter, Jill, cooked our main meal for us for 15 months at the cost of the extra workload on her as a wife and mother of two children whom she was home-schooling. My gratitude is very deep, and God's rewards to her will be great.

During the 12 ensuing years of daily pain (often severe) as Jim and I have sought the Lord for Him to say anything He desired concerning this bodily affliction, He has consistently spoken to us, mostly from His Word. I have journaled His responses and they make interesting and remarkable reading, particularly in the variety of ways He has repeatedly reiterated the same message.

1. He will miraculously heal me. (Medical science can do nothing for me. And I have tried numerous alternative methods for relief and am very involved in nutrition as a way of life.)

2. I need to keep on enduring with patience and unwavering faith, by appropriating God's grace.

3. The long delay is associated with a mentoring role as explained in James 2:5.

4. He will be greatly glorified as I wait with that strong desire for it to be so, and as I keep trusting Him for His perfect timing.

Five times in Deuteronomy we read that *"God spoke in the midst of the fire."* That is exactly my experience. I totally relate to the Scripture that says, *"Man shall not live by bread alone but by every word that proceeds from the mouth of God."* That has been, and continues to be my lifeline. I rest in the flawless character of the One who has graciously, faithfully, clearly, mercifully spoken to me consistently.

By far the biggest test is **the perplexity test**; by virtue of the extent of the pain and the length of the years of waiting for the fulfillment of God's many promises. Job's greatest tests were related to perplexity. Abraham's tests were related to the length of time he waited, and to the impossible-to-man promise. Joseph's tests were related to everything getting progressively worse the longer he waited. As my mobility has considerably decreased in recent years, I can now relate to all three men in some measure. Their lives are a great source of encouragement to me.

Before we look into what it means to experience the fellowship of Christ's sufferings by listing some of them, we need to hear what the apostle Peter has to say about it. He says that we are to rejoice to the extent that we are partaking of Christ's sufferings as part of the fiery trial, and that God's glory is going to be revealed, accompanied with exceeding joy. That's a significant and wonderful reward.

Our fiery ordeal, related to sharing Christ's sufferings (which is seldom taught or understood) can include any or all of the following circumstances, taken from the life of the Lord Jesus. Perhaps we'll recognize some of our own experiences.

• Being betrayed by a close friend (Judas).

- Being misjudged and misunderstood by close family members (His mother and brothers).
- Falsely accused by spiritual leaders (Pharisees).
- Denied by a friend (Peter).
- Entering into the pain of others' sufferings (John 11, with Martha and Mary at Lazarus' tomb).
- Weeping over the unfulfilled potential of others and the subsequent judgment (weeping over Jerusalem).
- Being ridiculed and humiliated by many (at His trial).
- Intense physical suffering (the scourging and crucifixion).
- The validity of His ministry being questioned by those who once acclaimed it (John the Baptist, His cousin).
- Having to be the mentor for others in relation to suffering (His intercessory ministry with forgiveness for Peter's denial, and those crucifying Him).
- At a time of greatest mental and emotional suffering when He most needed His closest friends, He reached out to them for help, but they failed to give it (Gethsemane).

If we have earnestly prayed Paul's prayer in Philippians 3:10, we shouldn't be surprised if we experience some or all of the above. After all, it's simply God answering our prayer to know Him. During these past 12 years of physical pain I was deeply wounded in my soul through being totally misjudged from a most unexpected source. No matter how I tried to explain my heart, it was not received as truth. A real measure of healing came from my receiving God's grace to completely forgive and unconditionally love the person. But that wasn't a new experience.

The thing that brought the greatest comfort in this perplexing situation was when I put together the above list of Jesus' sufferings as Son of Man. Only then did the Holy Spirit reveal to me that this particular suffering was directly connected to my having asked God numbers of times that I wanted to experience the fellowship of Christ's sufferings in order to more fully know Him. That understanding has brought a sense of privilege as well as enlightenment.

Because God's Word says that *"God vindicates the righteous,"* I knew I could trust my faithful Master to have the truth known in His way and time...even if it meant waiting for the Judgment Seat of Christ. In His infinite love and justice, God brought about circumstances outside my control, where I was fully vindicated and the relationship with the other party has become deeper and stronger. Praise God. As dear Dr. Robert Schuller would say, "God turned my scars into stars."

I love the way Eugene Peterson translates Second Corinthians 4:7-11 in *The Message* where Paul gives us his perspective on suffering. It's starkly real, but reveals how we live above our suffering as we keep our focus on the Lord Jesus at all times. I have proved these verses to be absolutely real.

We carry this precious Message around in the unadorned clay pots of our ordinary lives. That's to prevent anyone from confusing God's incomparable power with us. As it is, there's not much chance of that. You know for yourselves that we're not much to look at. We've been surrounded and battered by troubles, but we're not demoralized; we're not sure what to do, but we know that God knows what to do; we've been spiritually terrorized, but God hasn't left our side; we've been thrown down, but we haven't been broken. What they did to Jesus, they do to us—trial and torture, mockery and murder; what Jesus did among them, He does in us—He lives!

How I long that those of you who read this section of this book may receive some enlightenment and comfort in relation to the crucible of suffering you may be in. Anything that brings us closer to Jesus is rewarding—because Jesus is the most intriguing, exciting Being in the universe. He has totally captivated me, and is the only One who can totally fulfill me. If you have come this far in reading all of this book, you are probably just as passionate about Him! Or at least you want to be. If so—you will be.

Seeing the Big Picture

Living for eternity, not just this fleeting sojourn here on earth, helps to keep our focus in the most productive perspective. Everything we do here is just the school of preparation for the place of the big action—up there! God says some of us are going to rule nations in Heaven. We're hardly likely to be given that assignment if we haven't had world vision here on earth. That means, because of our obedience to God's priorities, our lives will effect every nation on earth. Psalm 67 says that the reason we've been blessed by God is that, *"His way may be known upon earth, His salvation among all nations."* It starts with systematically praying for every nation. You can read how to do that in my book, *Intercession, Thrilling and Fulfilling* (chapter 9), published by Y.W.A.M. Publishing.

Then, because of God's mandate to go into all the world and preach the gospel and make disciples, we need to be ready to be sent by God anywhere at any time under any conditions. It means being willing to be the answer to our prayers for the nations. That can include suffering. It also means being involved in giving our monetary resources to help evangelize the nations.

The apostle Peter puts the purpose for our suffering into the big picture of eternity when he writes, *"In this you greatly rejoice, though now for a little while, if need be, you have been grieved by various trials, that the genuineness of your faith, being much more precious than gold that perishes, though it is tested by fire, may be found to praise, honor and glory at the revelation of Jesus Christ"* (1 Peter 1:6-7). I love the way Pastor Warren Wiersbe translates these Scriptures. He states, *"Tried for a season. Pure for eternity. When God permits His children to go through the furnace, He keeps His eye on the clock and His hand on the thermostat. His loving heart knows how much and how long."* Now isn't that comforting!

One of the purposes of being subjected to the fire of God in suffering is to melt our hearts to make them more like His. We weep over many things under the Holy Spirit's moving upon our spirits.

- We weep over the things that grieve Him and bring Him sorrow. For example, disunity in His Body, or the lost souls of mankind.
- We weep over our sins—how they've hurt God and others, and immediately repent and make any restitution He requires.
- We weep in intercession as God shares His heart with us on behalf of others—their pain and suffering.
- We weep over those who are rebelling against God and are suffering the consequences.
- We weep when God encourages us—with relief and wonderment because He's the only one who knows how desperately we need it!!
- We weep in the presence of the Lord. The stronger the sense of His presence, the more broken and melted we are.
- We weep with the wonder of His mighty power when we see Him manifest it.

One of the purposes of natural fire is to give heat for life. It's a means for restoring healing and energizing. The same is true with the fire of God. It's interesting that so many of the reported instantaneous miracle healings today include the manifestation of supernatural heat in people's bodies.

When God's purposes are completed for sending or allowing the heat, He will turn on the fire of His power to deliver us, in His sovereign way and time. Our part is to be willing to endure until those purposes are completed. We're not in the fire of testing or persecution or suffering or temptation or purification to burn us up. We're there to be purified, made more pliable and beautiful (like gold being turned into jewelry), more Christlike.

In Numbers 31:21,23, we read about an ordinance of the Law which the Lord commanded Moses. *"Everything that can endure the fire, you shall put through the fire, and it shall be clean...but everything that cannot endure fire, you shall put through water."*

It's worth enduring the fire if we know we're coming out in far better shape than when we went in it. It helps us to embrace the fire as coming from God's loving hand when we understand one of the purposes is to cause our worship and praise to Him to be more acceptable. *"....He will purify the sons of Levi, and purge them as gold and silver that they may offer the Lord an offering in righteousness"* (Malachi 3:3).

The most encouraging verse I know in the Bible that assures us that one day when His purposes for our fiery trials are completed, He will give us the biggest breakthrough of all time. It's found in Isaiah 30:26: *"Moreover the light of the moon will be as the light of the sun, and the light of the sun will be sevenfold, as the light of seven days, in the day that the Lord binds up the bruise of His people and heals the stroke of their wound."*

The Fire of God in Temptation

Jesus, Our Model

One of the greatest aids in helping us navigate the turbulent perils of temptation is to understand that it's an integral part of being followers of Jesus. Our magnificent Master, Jesus, was in all points tempted as we are, yet without sin. That means that there is no temptation that we will ever face that He hasn't already experienced when on earth. It also means that He understands the tactics of the tempter and knows how to outsmart him. And as our great High Priestly intercessor, He knows how to most effectively pray to God the Father on our behalf, that we will come through the mine fields of carefully laid traps by the enemy, without being harmed.

As we study the life of the Lord Jesus, we find that His greatest times of temptation came straight after being baptized in water and being baptized in the Holy Spirit for empowering for ministry. (See Luke 3:21-22 and Luke 4:1-2.)

We should be warned and in turn warn others that we can expect our greatest temptations from the enemy of our souls to come after we've been empowered by the Holy Spirit for service.

In every military battle each side needs to understand the strengths and weaknesses of their opposing forces, as well as their own. Our captain, the Lord of Hosts, Jesus Christ, has never lost a battle. In fact, at the cross He triumphed over His foes, making an open show of them. Whereas our tempter, satan, is nothing but a fallen angel doomed to eternal destruction. There's nothing impressive about that status!

While satan has never even created as much as a toothpick, he's been around long enough to have some pretty subtle methods and means of tempting God's children. We need to wise up and understand his tactics. At the same time, because he's totally uncreative, we find that the tactics are the same old ones he tried out on Eve and Adam in the Garden of Eden. When you've lived through them and then watched him use the same ones on others, decade after decade, they become predictably boring. Pride and unbelief are the two main areas of attack, so that's where we need to be most on our guard.

One of the most subtle categories of temptation is in the area of deceit, which can be a mixture of truth and error. When satan was tempting Jesus to commit the sin of presumption by throwing Himself down from the pinnacle of the temple, he partially quoted a scripture from Psalm 91:11-12. Satan said, *"For it is written, "He shall give His angels charge over you, and in their hands they shall bear you up, lest you dash your foot against a stone."* He left out the words that followed *"for He gave His angels charge over you"* which were, *"to keep you in all your ways."* Jesus never acted independently of the Father, therefore *"His ways"* were only what the Father had ordered Him to do. Satan was tempting Jesus, through a partial quotation of Scripture to do His own thing. Jesus recognized this and said, *"It is written again, you shall not tempt the Lord your God."*

Satan's deception can be so strong that he has the power to actually cause a person to read a scripture and for that person to sincerely believe the exact opposite of what God is saying. I have had to counsel people in that condition. But I have also found that to those who are 100 percent sincerely seeking only truth, God will go to any lengths necessary to make sure that they ultimately have the truth revealed to them.

Then satan comes to tempt us in relation to things that appeal to our senses. He tempts us to indulge ourselves in ways that gratify our appetites, but are outside God's parameters for our well-being. They ultimately produce death in some form, not life.

After Jesus had fasted for 40 days and was hungry, satan tempted Him to rely on His nature of deity as Son of God, by making a stone become bread. But Jesus had chosen to put aside His nature of deity and function as Son of Man in total dependence upon the Father in all things. To have performed that miracle independently of the Father's orders would have been a violation of the purposes for which He came to earth, one of which was to show us how to live…in total submission, dependence, inquiry of the Father and obedience to Him in all things. That's why Jesus answered satan by saying, *"It is written, man shall not live by bread alone, but by every word that proceeds from the mouth of God"* (Matthew 4:4). Again satan was tempting Jesus to be presumptuous.

Then satan tempted Jesus to worship him. And I believe that's the most subtle of all suggestions. Because satanic forces can tempt us to put anyone or anything in the priority place of devotion above the Lord Jesus, which is called idolatry, he knows that if we succumb, we will ultimately not fulfill the purpose for which we were created. God is a jealous God and will never allow our lives to experience the fulfillment He intended if we have any other loves before Him.

We notice that two out of the three satanic temptations to the Lord Jesus related to presumption. As I have stated earlier in this book, I am convinced that the sin of presumption is one of the most deeply entrenched sins in the Body of Christ today. I would remind the reader that in Psalm 19:13, David cried out to God to be delivered from this sin, which he called "great transgression." How we need to see this sin as God sees it. Rev. Andrew Murray states that waiting on God is the forgotten art of the Church. I couldn't agree more. All presumption is rooted in pride. If you need help in understanding how to hear God's voice more clearly, in order to obey Him, you can obtain my book on that subject titled, *Forever Ruined for the Ordinary*. It has helped many in this area of need.

Weighing the Consequences

We sin because we choose to do so. The devil and other people's choices can tempt us to sin, but we choose what we do with that temptation. *"Let no one say when he is tempted, 'I am tempted by God's; for God cannot be tempted by evil, nor does He Himself tempt anyone. But each one is tempted when he is drawn away by his own desires and enticed. Then when desire has conceived, it gives birth to sin, and sin, when it is full grown, brings forth death"* (James 1:13-15).

It would be a wise safeguard to stop and answer the following questions when in the heat of temptation:

- What will be the consequences of my actions?
- Where will this take me? Where is it leading me?
- Is the gratification of this suggested desire really worth the price I will have to pay?
- Will it ultimately lead to producing life in me or some sort of destruction?
- Does this suggestion line up with God's Word or is it contrary to it?
- What does the Bible say about the consequences of what I am faced with doing?
- How will it affect the people nearest to me?
- How will it affect the circles of people whom I influence?
- Would I want others to know about what I am considering doing?
- Would I want present and future generations to know about and be affected by my choices at this time?
- Will my choices at this time bring me closer in relationship to the Lord Jesus or distance me from Him?

- Will my choices please the Lord and be used to extend His Kingdom, or please satan and help his cause?

Honest answers to the above questions would expose any deception from evil spirits, and enable us to avoid the wrong choices that inevitably produce pain and heartache to ourselves and others.

We can never say that the fires of temptation were too strong, or too subtle, or too different from what others have faced. Listen to the clarity and comfort of God's eternal Word. *"No temptation has overtaken you except such as is common to man; but God is faithful, who will not allow you to be tempted beyond what you are able, but with the temptation will also make a way of escape, that you may be able to bear it"* (1 Corinthians 10:13).

God allows temptations to come into our lives in order to see how we will react to them. But when we cry out to Him for help, not wanting to succumb to them, there's another wonderful verse that promises us deliverance: *"The Lord knows how to deliver the godly out of temptations"* (2 Peter 2:9). Our loving, understanding Lord Jesus has also promised special rewards for those who endure the fires of temptation. *"Blessed is the man who endures temptation; for when he has been approved, he will receive the crown of life which the Lord has promised to those who love Him"* (James 1:12).

Temptation to sin may come in many ways that we do not recognize, because of habit patterns. And those habits can have developed because we haven't yet had the revelation of God's reaction to them. A classic example would be the sin of murmuring and complaining.

The children of Israel were specialists in these sinful behavior patterns and tempted God on numerous occasions because of them. But there came a time when God wouldn't tolerate it anymore. First Corinthians 10:10 tells us that repeated sins of complaining resulted in their being destroyed. The Bible goes on to say, *"Now all these things happened to them as example, and they were written for our admonition...."*

So, what do we do about that warning? If we take God's Word seriously, we will be careful to check the words before they come out of our mouths, and more importantly, check the attitude of our hearts. I will illustrate.

This section of this lengthy book was one of the last I was working on. I was physically and mentally fatigued, late at night and in pain. Because that scenario was nothing new, and I had a desperate longing to get this marathon project to the place where I could submit it to the publishers...I was strongly tempted to complain about the heavy weight of responsibility and workload I've been carrying over many months to discharge God's mandate.

But I understood what was going on. God was watching and listening, and Jesus would be interceding for me. I had a choice. I chose to get into bed, put on worship tapes and for over an hour sang songs of worship and praise to God. Result? Perfect peace! No complaints!

The Safeguard of Humility

From many years of observation I have found that deception from the enemy in one form or another is usually found in those who used to be among the most dedicated disciples of the Lord Jesus.

How can this be?

Satan observes those who take God seriously, by their actions and words; especially those who frequently seek God's face and listen to His voice. The more obedient they are to God's directions, the more God rewards them with meaningful fulfillment. The Christian life has become an exciting adventure and these ones are what I call, ruined for the ordinary. They're out in orbit and have left the mundane world of doing their own thing far behind them. Inevitably they will stand out among the multitudes of ordinary Christians. That's often when satanic forces unleash their most subtle attacks upon the minds of those in this category. They go something like this.

"You're really different from most other Christians. In fact, I don't think there are many, or very few who hear God like you, and experience God like you." If there is the worst form of pride in that believer's heart, which is spiritual pride, the reaction to those suggestions will tend to be something like, "That's right. I really am operating on a plane that is superior to most, and therefore I am more important to God."

Whereas, if there is true humility in a believer's heart, the reaction would be something like this, "Those suggestions are simply not true, therefore they couldn't be coming from God. I believe multitudes of God's children have just as sincere a desire to hear God's voice and obey Him as I have." They would simply believe that when Jesus says in John 10: 3,4,27, *"My sheep hear My voice, know My voice and follow Me,"* that He would then fulfill His Word and communicate in some way to them. And besides, any suggestion that would make me feel superior to other believers would never be in accordance with God's Word. So, I resist the source of those impressions in the name of the Lord Jesus and the Word of God. It is written, *"Resist the devil and he will flee from you."* (James 4:7).

Satanic forces would get the message that there wasn't any point in trying to get a foothold and then a stronghold of deception in that believer's life because that person had chosen the pathway of humility. Satan is full of pride and knows nothing about humility. Therefore, humility is the greatest weapon against him. It floors him every time and outsmarts him. The Bible says, *"With the humble is wisdom."* Therefore satan has no wisdom. That's why he always overplays his hand. In Obadiah 3 we read, *"The pride of your heart has deceived you."* A Christian living in true biblical humility will never fall for the deceiver's lies. If any suggestion doesn't match up with God's standard of biblical holiness and humility from His Word, ***throw it out!***

The Strategy of Religious Spirits

Religious spirits are a mixture of deception and truth and are the most subtle of all demonic forces. They readily affirm the existence and need for a supreme divine being, called God, who is to be taken seriously. That's truth. The error is in not believing that Jesus Christ is part of the Godhead and is the only way we can come into a relationship with God the Father. The Bible says, *"There is one mediator between God and men, the man Christ Jesus"* (1 Timothy 2:5). To get people to deny the deity and resurrection of the Lord Jesus Christ is the fundamental strategy of all religious spirits. To believe that Jesus is part of the Trinity—God's sinless Son who paid the ultimate price for my redemption, and that He rose again, and by surrendering my will to Him, I come into a relationship with God as Father—makes me accountable to Jesus' claims upon my life. That's what religious spirits try to convince us against believing and acting on.

Religious spirits operate and flourish in and through religious people. They are characterized by having a zealous interest in spiritual things, and often quote Bible verses to support their convictions. They try to proselytize people by persuasive arguments, but have nothing to offer others that would cause them to have peace of mind coming from a change of heart, and subsequently a change of life.

They tend to be legalistic, with little concern or vision for reaching out to the world's needy—either spiritually, socially, or economically. They can talk philosophically about the world's needs but there is nothing to motivate them to become personally involved in meeting those needs.

In another category, millions are driven by fear, thinking that they have to earn the right to inherit divine favor by religious practices. Millions have never heard the truth about the only One who claimed to be, *"The Way, the Truth and the Life"* (John 14:6)—Jesus Christ. And who proved it by His supernatural life, death and resurrection. All they know to do to follow their God-given instinctive desire to worship, is to follow what has been presented to them as truth, usually from childhood. Religion is based upon regulations and rules and doesn't cause the individuals to have a change of heart. So self-striving, self-centeredness, and self-righteousness dominates their lives.

Given the opportunity of being exposed to the reality of Him who is the Way, the Truth and the Life, God's Son, the Lord Jesus Christ, many more are recognizing that all they have had was religion. Now they know and have a living, loving Savior and Redeemer who can forgive their sins and give them eternal life.

They gladly surrender their wills to Him and ask Him to come and live within their hearts according to God's invitations in the Bible. They experience a change of heart. As they daily invite the Holy Spirit to control their thoughts, words and actions, they discover their values in life change. Their desires and priorities change. Self-centeredness is replaced with Christ-centeredness. Their goal is to become like Him (see Romans 8:29). His priorities for their lives become their priorities by loving choices. God's love becomes the motivating force of their lives—more love for God, for His people, and for those who don't know Him.

Millions of religious people in this era of time have now become true disciples and followers of the Lord Jesus Christ. Fear has been replaced by faith and joy. Dogma has been replaced by truth and peace. Self-righteousness has been replaced by humility. Cold-hearted indifference has been replaced by the love of God. They no longer live for themselves but for Him who died for them and rose again (see 2 Corinthians 5:15). Satan, who is the mastermind behind all the religious spirits, has lost a big battle with these people because the Lord Jesus said, *"You shall know the truth and the truth shall set you free"* (John 8:32).

Pitfalls of Pride and Unbelief

Now there's another whole category of people who are under the control of religious spirits and deceiving spirits who need freeing by the fire of God's power. Their deception is a lot more subtle. Many of them have known the truth, even walked in it in varying degrees. But through intellectual pride have walked away from the simplicity of the truth. The Bible predicted this in Second Timothy 3:5 as *"having a form of godliness but denying it's power"* and verse 7, *"always learning and never able to come to the knowledge of the truth,"* and then in verse 13, they will be, *"deceiving and being deceived."*

The apostle Paul, writing to the young man Timothy, warned him about this state, explaining the necessity of believing in the inspired Word of God as the basis for his faith (see 2 Timothy 3:14-17).

"But you must continue in the things which you have learned and been assured of, knowing from whom you have learned them, and that from childhood you have known the Holy Scriptures, which are able to make you wise for salvation through faith which is in Jesus Christ. All Scripture is given by inspiration and is profitable for doctrine, for reproof, for correction, for instruction in righteousness, that the man of God may be complete, thoroughly equipped for every good work" (1 Timothy 3:14-17).

When we approach the reading of the Bible solely from our intellect, all we will gain is information. When we ask the Holy Spirit to illuminate our minds and teach us about God's character and ways from His Word, and believe that He will, we will receive revelation of truth. And revelation highly motivates us to obey the truth, which is the purpose for our having God's wonderful love letter to us, the Bible.

When intellectual pride takes over in our hearts and we become philosophical debaters about truth and not humble, diligent seekers of Truth (the Lord Jesus Christ Himself) then we become candidates for deceiving and religious spirits to take over and strongly influence our perspectives and convictions. These spirits are very aware that the greatest threat to their cause are humble, childlike Christians with a simple faith in an all-powerful, all-loving, all-wise, totally just, absolutely faithful and uncompromisingly holy God—Christians who realize their total dependence on Him at all times.

The main strategies of religious and deceiving spirits are aimed at appealing to our pride and unbelief. If they can convince people that (1) there is a plan for their lives that is more appealing than God's, and (2) that because of an elevated view of themselves they should pursue it, then they know they can convince them to change their course. It always starts in the mind. That's the battleground. And deception always includes compromising God's standards from His Word.

When Jesus was on earth, the religious leaders were classic examples of religious people being motivated by religious and deceiving spirits. Consequently, the righteous wrath of God was never more vehemently seen through the Lord Jesus than when He was addressing them—because God hates legalism, coldness of heart, judgmentalism, dishonesty, hypocrisy, and pride.

But there was an interesting exception among that religious hierarchy: Nicodemus. This leading, rabbinical teacher had an honest, humble heart that desperately wanted to know truth, diligently sought to find it, and finally did, as every honest seeker will. Nicodemus didn't fall for the satanic strategy of getting Temple-going religious leaders to deny the deity of the Son of God. Because Nicodemus wanted to genuinely learn from Jesus, and didn't envy Him, the deceiver couldn't gain a foothold on his mind.

Now let's look at another religious zealot among the religious hierarchy at the beginning of the Church: Saul of Tarsus. Wow! Was he ever taken over by religious spirits! They always have an intolerance to radically real sold-out disciples of the Lord Jesus, and Saul was no exception. Saul was driven by the ultimate deceiver, the father of lies, satan, to drag the Christians from their homes and throw them into prison.

It is interesting to note that both Nicodemus and Saul were exposed to the same rabbinical school of learning. Both were steeped in the knowledge of Hebrew laws and traditions. Both were recognized as scholars of much learning. Then why did they act with such opposite reactions when confronted with the Truth (Jesus)? It had to be because of the different state of their hearts. You may say, "But Saul didn't have the same opportunity to see Jesus as Nicodemus did." Not the same opportunity, but certainly a great opportunity.

It was because of the early Christians' intense devotion to the Lord Jesus Christ and their desire for others to know Him that they were suffering so greatly at the hands of Saul. Saul was exposed to the life of Christ in these precious, devoted disciples of Jesus every time he badly mistreated and threatened to murder them, which was daily. He had witnessed Stephen the martyr being stoned with his face shining like an angel and heard him pray, *"Lord, do not charge them with this sin"* (Acts 7:60). Saul had certainly been exposed to the life of Jesus Christ in powerful ways.

Proverbs 16:18 says, *"Pride goes before destruction and a haughty spirit before a fall."* God knew what it would take to make this Christ-opposer who was impressed with all his learning, intellectual attainments, religious background, and religious zeal into the humble bond slave of Jesus Christ that he later became. It started with being knocked off his horse as the fire of God's power struck him, and God rebuked him in an audible voice from heaven. The glory of God, in the strength of the light that shone on him, blinded his eyes and he had to be led by the hand by others.

Pride is the basis of all deception. *"The pride of your heart has deceived you"* (Nahum 3). Whereas humility is the basis of wisdom. *"When pride comes, then comes shame; but with the humble is wisdom"* (Proverbs 11:2). Jesus kept using little children as examples of how our hearts are to be in order to please Him: simple, transparently honest, trusting, loving, and dependent on Him. The apostle Paul became all that and was profoundly used of God to expose religious and deceiving spirits and to free people from them. Humility made the difference.

Freedom From Deception

No one needs to remain under the influence of deceiving spirits. First John 3:8 says that *"for this purpose the Son of God was manifested that He might destroy the works of the Devil."* And Jesus said, *"Behold, I have given you authority...over all the power of the enemy"* (Luke 10:19).

For example, when a person discerns that a deceiving spirit is operating, either through themselves or someone else, the first thing is to recognize how the demonic spirit was able to gain a foothold in that person's life.

As we have previously seen from God's Word in Nahum verse 3, un-dealt-with pride is the cause of deception. Many times, spiritual pride has come from not giving God the glory when God has been using a person in some special way. The more God uses us, the more easily we can become impressed with ourselves instead of being convinced of the following truths:

Psalm 62:11: *"God has spoken once, twice I have heard this; that power belongs to God."*
Isaiah 48:11: *"....I will not give My glory to another."*
And in John 15:5: *"Without Me you can do nothing (spiritual)."*
Proverbs 16:11: *"Everyone proud in heart is an abomination to the Lord. Though they join forces, none will go unpunished."*

To illustrate how the most sincere Christian can become ensnared by deception and then freed, I share the following story.

I knew a devout Christian who came into this category; loved and respected by many, and who went to be with the Lord a number of years ago. He became aware during times when ministering to others that sometimes the impressions he received were obviously from the Holy Spirit, but other times they were not. This puzzled and disturbed him because this servant of the Lord feared God and was committed to the truth at all times. He began to wonder if at times he was under the influence of a deceiving spirit. He set aside three days to fast and pray for God to reveal to him the cause of these false impressions that sometimes came to his mind. He was aware that they could have come from his own mind as well as from the enemy, but he knew that God knew the true source, and was confident that He would reveal the truth to him.

On the second day, God confirmed to him that his wonderings about being influenced by deceiving spirits were correct, and in genuine brokenness he deeply repented of the sin of spiritual pride that God revealed to him was the cause of the enemy gaining a foothold in his life. In obedience to the promptings of the Holy Spirit, he took authority over the spirit of deception, in the all-powerful name of the Lord Jesus, commanding it to cease to influence him and not to return, on the basis of Jesus' shed blood on the cross, quoting the Scriptures from Revelation 12:11 and James 4:7. He then declared in faith, *"Thanks be to God who gives us the victory through our Lord Jesus Christ."* He was totally freed by the fire of God's power, and never again was troubled in the area of deception.

It was a tremendous lesson to him, and underlined again to us with whom he humbly shared his experience, that un-dealt-with spiritual pride can open us up to demonic influences, regardless of how long we've walked with the Lord or how greatly He has used us to bless others. Pride was the cause. Humility was the first step to freedom. It always is. *"God gives grace to the humble"* (1 Peter 5:5).

How to Overcome Temptation

I am totally convinced from God's Word and from my own experience that by far the greatest immunization against the fiery darts of satanic temptation, whatever the category, in whatever position or condition we're in is ***the fear of the Lord.*** Why? Because of its definition. *"The fear of the Lord is to hate evil"* (Proverbs 8:13).

We sin because we choose to sin. We have free will. Sin is presented in some form to us, and we choose, by committing it, to do what we know we shouldn't, or by omission, to not do what we should. We make one of those choices when the temptation is presented to us. We have our first reaction in our thought life. Our choices are determined by whether or not there is a love for sin or a hatred of sin in our hearts. Because the fear of God is to *hate* evil, obviously it is our greatest overcoming agent in relation to sin. We don't choose to do the things we hate. We avoid them like the plague.

Conversely, we choose to do the things we love. That brings us to the moments of stark honesty where we need to state the obvious. "The reason I…[state the sin]…was because I loved that sin and didn't hate it. I obviously need a change of *heart* over that sin." Thank God, He has the answer and will faithfully give us as much of the fear of the Lord as we want to ask for, and receive by faith. That's not complicated.

We may not feel a thing when we pray those prayers, but I can guarantee you, as surely as night follows day, that every time we pray them in sincerity and faith, God will change our entire attitude toward that sin.

How will we know for sure? By the way we will instinctively respond to the next time temptation comes to us in relation to that sin. It will be distasteful to us. The pleasure associated with it has been removed. *"By the fear of the Lord a man avoids evil"* (Proverbs 16:6). What we once loved, we now hate. In time, satan gets the message and sees the futility of bringing temptation to us in those areas that are saturated with the fear of the Lord. That's real freedom!

If sin fascinates us in any way, even if we don't commit it, we will know there is a need for the fear of the Lord in that area of our lives. Because Jesus was devoted to the fear of the Lord, as prophesied by Isaiah, long before Jesus' birth, He could say, *"for the ruler of this world is coming but he has nothing in Me"* (John 14:30). In other words, nothing that satan could tempt Him with had any place in Jesus' life because it had no appeal to Him, only distaste. That's freedom to walk the highway of holiness that Isaiah refers to in Isaiah 35:8. He says, *"The unclean shall not pass over it, but it shall be for others."* If you're often bombarded with satanic suggestions to your mind, ask God to reveal to you the platform of un-repented-of sin in your life with which you need to deal.

To be forewarned is to be forearmed. I received a letter from a married woman who listened to my teaching tapes on the fear of the Lord. She was particularly helped by my explaining that in our relationships with the opposite sex we can experience attractions in any or all of the following areas: physical attraction, personality compatibility, mental affinity, and spiritual unity. I went on to explain that when God tests us in the area of holiness of life, He may put us alongside someone in ministry with one or all of those attractions. If that person is outside God's boundaries in relation to being married to them, because of God's other plan for our lives and theirs, we need to be clothed with the fear of the Lord in thought, word, and action regarding that relationship. As spiritual unity is the strongest attraction of the four, we need to be particularly on our guard against the enemy's wiles.

The woman wrote to me explaining that she had prayerfully passed the tests related to the first three attractions but had never been tested in the area of spiritual unity with another man. Because of the deficiency in her own marriage in this area, and her very deep desires to have fulfillment, she realized how extremely vulnerable she would be if faced with this kind of temptation. In her own words she wrote, "Joy, I will tell you truthfully before God, I'm afraid it would have completely thrown me. I may have deceived myself and tried to rationalize something from it that I wanted because of my own heart's unfulfilled desire. As I heard you teach on this, I knew in my heart that this was an area that I must protect at all cost. I am going to fortify it with the fear of the Lord, so if I ever face this temptation I will know how to respond." Just one testimony like that is worth all the effort that goes into having a Bible teaching ministry.

You may be thinking, "I have failed. I've fallen for satan's lies," or "I chose to disobey God's Word to gratify my own desires. What hope is there for me?" God's mercy is always extended to a sincerely repentant heart. God not only promises to forgive us from present and past sins, but promises us great hope for the future. *"Sanctify yourselves, for tomorrow the Lord will do wonders among you"* (Joshua 3:5).

He is always the God of tomorrow, regardless of yesterday's failures. Isn't it wonderful that He goes beyond forgiving us when we have sinned, and actually promises us that in His time, He will use us mightily if we will truly repent? What a God!

God can turn our greatest failures into the greatest successes if we will fully cooperate with Him—to the point where satanic forces will be very sorry that they ever messed with us! Or, God will use the very thing that was the cause of our potential destruction to become the thing, in God's hands, that He will use to display His miracle-working power.

I loved hearing the way Dr. Charles Stanley illustrated this timeless truth that I have taught for many years. He explained that it happened when Peter and the other disciples were in a severe storm, on the sea, out in a little boat, late at night. Peter actually walked on the water, which was the substance that had the potential danger of destroying him and his friends. Every time we go God's way, even after failure, it causes the devil and his demons to become frustrated, confused, and defeated. Now, that's enough reason to throw a praise party!

THE FIRE OF GOD'S GLORY

In this section we are going to see how God manifests the fire of His glory in a variety of ways and at times when we would expect it the least. The glory of God is the sum total of all God's characteristics. Only in our glorified bodies in Heaven will we be able to stay in God's presence and see Him as He is for unlimited lengths of time and not be consumed by the intensity of His Being.

The fire of God's glory was manifest as a means of God's directions to the children of Israel as we see in Exodus 13:21: *"And the Lord went before them by day in a pillar of cloud to lead the way, and by night in a pillar of fire to give them light."* This was a continuous manifestation of God's goodness and glory among His people. Then, when Pharaoh's armies were almost breathing down the Israelites' necks and were about to overtake them at the Red Sea, God ordered His angel who was in charge of the pillar of cloud to switch positions and go behind God's people to act as a smoke screen to protect them from their enemies. How's that for ingenuity! What a fabulous, caring, protective God! And He's in business to equally care for His own today, and He hasn't run out of unheard-of ways to do it. In fact, He's the ultimate specialist in that business.

Recently, an Iraqi pastor's wife who was working with the Russian Embassy was walking around the streets of Baghdad. As was her habit, she was memorizing Scripture. The wind was blowing very hard. As she approached a small shop where some construction work was being done, suddenly a large sheet of plywood and boards nailed together started to fall on her at a 45-degree angle. She cried out to God for protection. Inexplicably there was a sudden wind change of 180 degrees, which caused the piece of the construction to reverse its downfall, enabling that Christian woman to walk under it to safety, only brushing her arm which she had raised for protection. Just as suddenly, the wind changed direction again and the boards crashed to the ground.

We need to understand that the fire of God's glory can be manifest in both blessing and judgment. In Numbers 16 we read about Korah, Dathan, Abiram, and On, four leading men among the Israelites who led 250 other well-known leaders in a mutiny against Moses and Aaron, severely criticizing and judging them wrongly.

God's reaction was to manifest the glory of the Lord to all the congregation (see Numbers 16:18). But it was anything but a sign of His approval, because the next order God gave was to tell Moses and Aaron to separate themselves from among the congregation that He may consume them in a moment. It was only because Moses and Aaron fell on their faces and interceded for the congregation's lives to be spared that God reversed His orders by instructing Moses to tell everyone to separate themselves from the mutinous leaders (see Numbers 16:24). Then God went into action.

These four men found themselves with the ground splitting under them and being swallowed up alive as their screams rent the air. Then a fire came out from the Lord and consumed the other 250 rebellious men. We see from this account that the glory of the Lord appearing among the people was a sign that He had showed up, but not with His approving presence.

In Numbers 14, we again see the glory of God being manifest at a time we would least expect. After the men had given a bad report to the children of Israel after having spied out the land of Canaan, the people embarked on an all-out murmuring and complaining campaign against Moses and Aaron. It was a bad scene.

The people questioned God's character, suggested returning to Egypt and even proposed selecting another leader in order to do so. Heavy drama ensued! Moses and Aaron had their predictable humility reaction by falling on their faces before God as intercessors for the rebellious mob. Joshua and Caleb tore their clothes and gave their version (and God's) of what the Israelites should do. They exhorted the people not to rebel against the Lord and strongly urged them with encouraging words to not be afraid but to trust and obey God and enter Canaan.

The Israelites' reaction was violent. They planned to stone these men of God who had spoken the truth to them. ***Then God showed up—center stage—with a display of His glory!*** Ignoring the people, God conversed with Moses, announcing His plan to strike the people with diseases and to disinherit them, while starting over again by making a mightier nation with Moses.

God expressed His dismay over the Israelites' rejection of His rulership and blatant unbelief, despite the fact that they had repeatedly witnessed the incredible signs and wonders God had performed on their behalf. Moses' response as an intercessor is unsurpassed in human history, and his boldness can only be explained by the depth and intimacy of his knowledge of God's character. His greatest concern was for God Himself, not the rebellious people he led, and certainly not himself. The main thrust of this historic dialog with the Almighty was to draw His attention to the fact that the other nations would conclude that God didn't have what it took to fulfill His promises to get His people to their destination, so He killed them. God would appear to be weak.

However, it is very significant to note that Moses' most compelling argument was that the Egyptians knew the fire of God's glory appeared to God's people every morning and evening. And that God had spoken to their leader face to face (verse 14) as well as demonstrating God's awesome power in unheard of ways to man. Because of all this, the Egyptians would tell the other nations that Israel's God is not such a big deal after all. He caved in and gave up on His project, so we can forget about being so awestruck about Him. In other words, they will say that the manifest presence of God displayed in the fire of His glory, couldn't have been that impressive after all.

Now, we must understand that the only way Moses, or anyone else can talk to God like that is because the Spirit of God was working in and through him. *"For it is God who works in you both to will and to do of His good pleasure"* (Philippians 2:13). No one therefore, would have been more pleased, and the least surprised with Moses' response to God, than God Himself. Moses then went on to plead the other aspects of God's character to God, by appealing to God's longsuffering and unending mercy, while totally understanding and agreeing with His holiness and judgment. All this explains why Moses was called God's friend. The closer the friendship the more understanding of that person's character.

God's response to His close friend was in the classic words, "I have pardoned according to your word" (verse 20). But that is only half the sentence. In verse 21, God goes on to make this amazing statement. *"But truly as I live, **all the earth shall be filled with the glory of the Lord.**"*

I believe God is making the point that despite how humanity messes up on God's intended plans for them, there will come a day when God will display His consummate glory by a show of all His characteristics. His name and character will be totally vindicated in Heaven and earth and under the earth. That's when every knee shall bow and every tongue will confess that Jesus Christ is Lord to the glory of God the Father.

Finally, God displays His justice and judgment alongside His compassion and mercy by pronouncing that all those who rejected His rulership would die in the wilderness over the course of their lifespan and not enter Canaan, while all those 20 years old and under would enter as promised.

While God can extend mercy to us by our not getting what we deserve, we must always remember that we will reap what we sow. It is a spiritual law. Sin has its consequences. At the same time, to the depth and extent of our repentance and humbling ourselves, the sentence of reaping will be shortened (see Micah 7:18-19).

The fire of God's glory can be so awesome in its intensity that it can be overwhelming. The fire of God, the glory of God, and the power of God are closely linked in Scripture. And the combination can be unbearably intense. In Second Chronicles 7:1-3, following a protracted time of intercession when the fire of God supernaturally came down from Heaven on the burnt offerings and sacrifices, the priests were totally unable to function in their ministries inside God's house because of the intensity of the glory of God that followed. All the people could do outside was to fall on their faces on the ground in praise and worship.

In Isaiah 2:5, the prophet Isaiah calls God's people to *"walk in the light of the Lord."* That simply means to live according to God's standard of holiness found in His Word. He then exposes the sins of idolatry that are manifest through materialism. Throughout this section there are seven strong references to God's actions in humbling everyone who is proud. Pride is always the cause of all idolatry—everything that we place of importance more than an ardent pursuit of God Himself.

Two verses say, in essence, exactly the same thing. *"The loftiness of man shall be bowed down, and the haughtiness of men shall be brought low. The Lord alone will be exalted in that day"* (Isaiah 2:11,17). That's God's radical, revolutionary revolt against man's greatest sin!

There are also three verses that give us a preview of what a display of God's glory will produce throughout the earth. *"They shall go into the holes of the rocks, and into the caves of the earth, from the terror* [or violent power] *of the Lord and the glory of His majesty* [or awesome presence]" (Isaiah 2:10,19,21).

Unfortunately, we all too seldom hear Bible teaching on these aspects of the fire of God's glory, highlighting the fact that one of our greatest needs is a far greater understanding of God's character and ways. Psalm 104:4 says God makes His ministers a flame of fire. I believe we have little understanding and even less experience of the implications of that statement. To illustrate, I will quote from George Stormont's book, *Smith Wigglesworth: A Man Who Walked With God.*

In 1922, when Smith Wigglesworth was ministering in Wellington, New Zealand, he called for a special prayer meeting with a group of eleven leaders. After each of them had prayed, Wigglesworth rose to seek the Lord, and the presence of God began to fill the room. Soon the glory of God became terrible. The light became too bright, the heat too intense. The other men couldn't take it any longer. Every one of them left the room. Only Smith Wigglesworth could continue in the *Shekinah* [Glory of God].

Another minister heard what had happened and determined at the next gathering, no matter how strong the presence of God became, he would stay until the end. Once again the holy presence of God filled the room and the glory became unbearable. Everyone left except this one leader. He would not be overcome and driven out by the manifest presence of the Lord. But it was too much. Wigglesworth was caught up in the Spirit, radiant with holy fire, and even the determined minister couldn't stand the intensity. Soon enough he was gone too.[42]

Do we really want to experience the intensity of God's fire and glory?

God wants to trust us more with the dynamic power of His authority through us in ministry to others, whether hidden in intercession or public, whether one-on-one or to multitudes. *"How great is God— beyond our understanding" (Job 36:26). "Who can understand the thunder of His power?"* (Job 26:14)

Charles Spurgeon, known as "the prince of preachers," prayed: *God, send us a season of glorious disorder. Oh for a sweep of the wind that will set the seas in motion and make our ironclad brethren, now lying so quietly at anchor, to roll from stem to stern! Oh for the fire to fall again—fire which will affect the most solid! Oh that such a fire might first sit on the disciples, and then fall on all around! Oh God, You are ready to work with us today even as You did then. Stay not, we beseech You, but work at once. Break down every barrier that hinders the incoming of Your might! Give us now both hearts of flame and tongues of fire to preach Your reconciling word, for Jesus' sake. Amen.[43]*

If we want to be trusted with the fire of God's glory through us, we will have to subjected to the same fire to burn out everything that is not Christlike. Amy Carmichael, that wonderful, Christ-like, woman missionary to the people of India, understood that truth, and put it in the following prayer. "Give me the love that leads the way, the faith that nothing can dismay, the hope no disappointments tire, the passion that will burn like fire, let me not sink to be a clod; Make me Thy fuel, Flame of God."[44]

The following testimony from Kathy Gray vividly illustrates this truth. It is taken from the *Women of Destiny Bible* (NKJV), published by

Thomas Nelson Bibles, and is being used with their permission. By the way, this unique and remarkable Bible is laced with powerful teachings and testimonies from women of God who have proved the truths in God's precious Word. It also has many pertinent nuggets of truth from well-known men of God. I use it frequently and highly recommend it.

For me, bitterness and pride formed a stranglehold on my personality most of my life. This became the "taproot" of my personality, feeding every other attitude. After so many years of nurturing this root, I became the "professional" minister, pretending to have the fire of God. My passion for Jesus was being snuffed out.

I could teach other women the "Scriptural Formula for Freedom From Bitterness," but I was not free. Fasting and prayer only suppressed this taproot before it would spring up again. Whenever I would get close to true repentance and change, self-justification would rise up, quenching my freedom. This vicious cycle dulled me, making me ineffective as a believer. I needed fire, not a formula! I needed a direct encounter with God's burning presence. I needed Him to do something in me that was beyond my self-effort.

In the midst of a mighty outpouring of the Holy Spirit in our church, I would watch while other women were supernaturally touched by God's fire. Yet, fear mixed with pride held me back from receiving. My husband finally told me with tears in his eyes, "You're going to miss your destiny if you don't yield to the glory of God."

By then I was desperate to experience God intensely. My pride and body ended up on the floor as I heard women praying, "Jesus, plunge your hand in Kathy's soul and free her from this taproot of bitterness and pride!" As I yielded to the fire of God, I felt the weightiness of His glory on me and a burning within me. Lasting freedom came! At my burning bush, my destiny was restored. It was an intimate time where the Lord consumed my lifelong stranglehold.

My prayer for you is that you will meet face-to-face with the power of God and allow Him to do what you cannot do on your own. May He consume all that is not of Him and replace it with His fire.

The Refiner's Fire

He sits by a furnace of sevenfold heat
As He watches by the precious ore.
Closer He bends with a searching gaze
As He heats it more and more.
For He knows He has ore that can stand the test
And He wants the finest gold
To mold as a crown for the King to wear
Set with gems of price untold.
So He lays our gold in the burning fire,
Tho' we fain would say to Him "Nay"
And He watches the dross that we could not see,
As it melts and passes away.
The gold grows brighter and brighter it grows,
And our eyes grow dim with tears,
We see but the fire... not the Master's hand,
And question with anxious fears
Yet our gold shines out with a richer glow
As it mirrors a form from above
That bends o'er the fire tho' unseen by us,
With a look of ineffable love.
Can we think it pleases His loving heart
To cause us a moment's pain?
Ah, no! but He sees through the present cross
The bliss of eternal gain.
So He waits there with a watchful eye,
With a love that is strong and sure,
And His gold did not suffer a bit more heat
Than was needed to make it pure.

~Author unknown

SURVIVING THE FIRE
WITHOUT BEING BURNED

I am aware that a smattering of what I will be sharing in this closing section has been touched on before in different parts of this book. My thinking is that it could be helpful to capsulize the basics of how to react to the different aspects of the fire of God. After all, I guess that was one of the main purposes in God's heart when He directed me to write on this subject.

God has promised in Isaiah 43:2 that when we walk through the fire we shall not be burned, nor shall the flame scorch us. The following truths give understanding how that promise can be fulfilled.

1. **By having the revelation of the character of God, which only comes from having studied it, facet by facet from His Word—especially His love, His justice, and His faithfulness.** The longer God keeps us in the fire and the hotter the flames, these are the attributes of God we'll be most tempted to doubt. When God allows us to be stripped of everything, and there's absolutely nothing left for us to depend on but His character, we had better have in-depth revelation,

because in the greatest heat of the fiery trial, God can purposely withdraw all other understanding.

My faith may have wavered had I not taken much time to study God's character as a way of life. I had nothing left to cling to, or hang my faith on, when in the furnace of affliction and we can be so ill, we're incapable of discerning His voice.

The greatest test of all is the perplexity test. In every other trial I could always explain God's character and ways related to the circumstances where 2+2=4. This trial of physical affliction has been characterized by 2+2=57 most of the time! Perplexing and discouraging circumstances have been frequent and continual. Paul says he was perplexed but not in despair in Second Corinthians 4:8. So I'm in good company. During this illness I've had four accidents, three of which have brought prolonged pain to other parts of my body, with no understanding from God as to why they were allowed. I have a deeper appreciation of Romans 11:33: *"O the depth of the riches and knowledge of God. How unsearchable are His judgments and His ways past finding out."* But my faith hasn't failed, because the revelation of God's character is stronger than anything that has been hurled at me to convince me otherwise.

Also, all throughout the continued pain, weakness, sleeplessness, and perplexities, on numerous occasions God has faithfully brought me the exact message I needed to hear on Christian TV or a taped message, or a book, or a letter, or a poem from sensitive, caring friends. The timing of these love gifts from God has been an incredible display of His tenderness and infinite understanding. Truly, *"God is just in all His ways and kind in all His doings"* (Psalm 145:17). God's love has been manifest more strongly to me through my precious husband Jim, than perhaps in any other way. There are no words to adequately describe the depth of my love and gratitude to him. I often find myself calling him, "Angel."

We are warned in God's Word that if we try to take matters into our own hands, by forming our own conclusions and making our own decisions when we are in perplexing situations, we will land in big trouble. *"Who among you fears the Lord? Who obeys the voice of His Servant? Who walks in darkness and has no light? Let him trust in the name of the Lord and rely upon his God. Look, all you who kindle a fire, who encircle yourselves with sparks: walk in the light of your fire and in the sparks you have kindled—this you shall have from My hand: you shall lie down in torment"* (Isaiah 50:10-11).

It always pays to keep trusting God's unswerving faithfulness, infinite wisdom and knowledge, absolute justice and unfathomable love, no matter how dark and perplexing the circumstances. He hasn't abdicated His throne, is in total control, and knows your address.

2. **We need to discipline our thoughts to keep focusing on the Lord Jesus throughout the day.** We need to express our love and thanks to Him frequently and tell Him we trust Him. Our faith is dependent upon, and controlled by, our focus and "looking unto Jesus" (Hebrews 12:2). We are Christ-centered in direct proportion to how automatically we relate our everyday circumstances to the Lord Jesus Christ. David says in Psalm 16:8-9: *"I have set the Lord always before me; because He is at my right hand I shall not be moved."* This means being preoccupied with God.

3. **To survive the fire and not be burned we choose to praise and worship God vocally as a way of life.** *"I will bless the Lord at all times; His praise shall continually be in my mouth"* (Psalm 34:1).

It will not only keep our focus and perspective right, but it may well keep our sanity, it did mine. It's also a powerful means of spiritual warfare. *"Now when they began to sing and to praise, the Lord set ambushes against the people of Ammon, Moab and Mount Seir, who had come against Judah; and they were defeated"* (2 Chronicles 20:22). *"Let the saints be joyful in glory; let them sing aloud on their beds. Let the high praises of God be in their mouth and a two edged sword in their hand"* (Psalm 149:5-6).

4. **Engage daily in spiritual warfare as directed in Ephesians 6:10-18:**

   Finally, my brethren, be strong in the Lord and in the power of His might. Put on the whole armor of God, that you may be able to stand against the wiles of the devil. For we do not wrestle against flesh and blood, but against principalities, against powers, against the rulers of the darkness of this age, against spiritual hosts of wickedness in heavenly places. Therefore take up the whole armor of God that you may be able to withstand in the evil day, and having done all to stand. Stand therefore, having girded your waist with truth, having put on the breastplate of righteousness and having shod your feet with the preparation of the gospel of peace; above all, taking the shield of faith with which you will be able to quench all the fiery darts of the wicked one. And take the helmet of salvation, and the sword of the Spirit, which is the word of God; praying always with all prayer and supplication in the Spirit, being watchful to this end with all perseverance and supplication for all the saints.

   Young David took the initiative in his battle with Goliath by declaring his faith in the name of the Lord of hosts. Then David hurried and ran to meet the Philistine giant. (See First Samuel 17:48.)

   Either the devil is harassing us, or we're harassing him. Be on the offensive daily, and resist him in Jesus' name before he can attack us. And in First Peter 5:8-9: *"Be sober, be vigilant; because your adversary the devil walks about like a roaring lion, seeking whom he may devour. Resist him, steadfast in the faith, knowing that the same sufferings are experienced by your brotherhood in the world."*

When we walk in the fear of the Lord, we don't fear men or devils. They fear us.

5. **It is important to pray regularly for others who are suffering, and to keep being obedient to all the priorities God shows us.** It's the only pathway to fulfillment and blessing. See Deuteronomy 28:1-15. *"Chosen and destined by God the Father and sanctified by the Spirit for obedience to Jesus Christ"* (1 Peter 1:2).

6. **Realize we can't go through the fiery trial without the help, prayers, encouragement, and comfort of others.** If we think we can, then God may well make it hotter until we know we can't. So decide now to be open to declare your weakness and call for help. Jesus did, three times in the garden of Gethsemane. He asked for prayer support from some of His closest friends when He was facing the agonies of being separated from His Father during the times of His greatest need. This included becoming sin for all sinners, while enduring the excruciating pain of crucifixion.

   Paul did during his imprisonment. *"For I know this will turn out for my salvation through your prayer and the supply of the Spirit of Jesus Christ"* (Philippians 1:19). And in Colossians 4:3-4, Paul calls for prayer support, mentioning his chains—and also in verse 18: *"remember my chains."* Those chains represented suffering and long confinement. Paul knew that he needed the prayers of others to help him endure with patience until God's time for his release.

7. **To survive the fire and not be burned, keep in God's precious Word.** David said, *"Your testimonies also are my delight and my counselors"* (Psalm 119:24). In fact, David said that if it hadn't been for his delighting in God's Word, he would have perished in his affliction (see Psalm 119:92).

It is very beneficial to meditate on First Peter 1:6-7 and James 1:2-4. They tell us to be encouraged and be glad that we'll come through the fire in better shape than when we went in, if we cooperate with God's purposes.

Wherever else you're reading in the Bible, make sure you stay in the Psalms. That's the concentrated record of those who made it through the fire. They speak the language of our hearts, which brings identification, comfort, hope, and faith.

A dichotomy may well take place in your thinking. God tells us directly from His Word to rest in Him and wait patiently and trust in Him without any or little understanding of what's going on. Jesus said, *"What I am doing you do not understand now, but you will after this"* (John 13:7), and *"This poor man cried out and the Lord heard him, and saved him out of all his troubles"* (Psalm 34:6).

Parallel to that, we'll find ourselves seeking Him diligently for more understanding, and doing our best to believe His many promises for deliverance and healing. *"Many are the afflictions of the righteous but the Lord delivered him from them all"* (Psalm 34:19).

Both truths are complementary to each other. We keep seeking God for greater understanding of His character and ways and anything He wants to say to us. When He speaks, we obey. We never limit Him through unbelief. At the same time we rest in His flawless character, and trust Him to perfect that which concerns us. *"The Lord will perfect that which concerns me; Your mercy, O Lord, endures forever; do not forsake the works of Your hands"* (Psalm 138:8).

8. **When we are hurting the most, and there's little or no change and the temptation to discouragement is strong, we can always cry out to God for a special *Rhema word* of encouragement from His Word.** This becomes our lifeline and diffuses discouragement: *"Man shall not live by bread*

alone, but by every word that proceeds from the mouth of God" (Matthew 4:4).

"The Lord spoke out of the midst of the fire" is repeated four times in Deuteronomy 4:33; 5:4; 5:22; 5:26.

Don't let God go. Persist until He speaks to you personally in your fire. Write it down, believe it, and hang on to it in faith and talk it back to God. I've lost count of the number of times God has spoken to Jim and me from His Word that I'll be healed. And I've needed every single verse, every time. *"Remember the word to Your servant, upon which You have caused me to hope. This is my comfort in my affliction, for Your Word has given me life"* (Psalm 119:49-50).

We can also ask God to send us specific Rhema words from Himself through reliable, trusted sources as well, for confirmation. My testimony, along with David's, is Psalm 119:92: *"Unless Your law had been my delight, I would have perished in my affliction."* God doesn't mind how many times we come back asking for encouragement. Because, *"He is touched with the feeling of our infirmities"* and *"He knows our frame and remembers we are but dust"* (Hebrews 4:15). Remember, Jesus was *"a man of sorrows and acquainted with grief"* and knows all about the dark night of the soul. He couldn't understand why the depth of suffering had to be so great, when He cried out on the cross, *"My God, My God why have You forsaken Me?"* He couldn't say "My Father," because He was being made sin for us, and therefore was under God's judgment, which severed Their fellowship during those horrendous hours.

The outcome of our seeking God will be, as recorded in Zechariah 13:9b: *"They will call upon My name and I will answer them."* (He will come through and speak to us.) We then believe Him and trust Him. God will then say proudly, *"This is My people,"* and each one will say, *"The Lord is my God,"* in submission, praise, and worship.

9. **If God reveals to you that these difficult circumstances are mainly connected with the trial of your faith, including the fellowship of His sufferings, then believe that God is controlling the heat of the flames and trust Him.** You'll see Him sovereignly adjust the temperature according to His divine purpose, not because He's capricious or whimsical. He's revealing to you that He understands your circumstances. He's in control. I have witnessed this truth on numerous occasions, and when the pain has sovereignly and temporarily lifted I have always seen God's purposes in doing so. It's been truly remarkable.

   Recently when I was asking God, "Is this prolonged suffering basically the trial of my faith?" The answer came as follows:

   - See Matthew 15:21-28. When Jesus delayed to answer the repeated requests of the Canaanite woman for her daughter's deliverance, she was being tested on her humility, persistency, and faith.
   - The Holy Spirit spoke to me, "Turn to page 568 in your Bible." It turned out to be Proverbs 17:3: *"The refining pot is for silver and the furnace for gold, but the Lord tests the hearts"* (testing of my faith).
   - Luke 22:31-32: *"Satan has desired to sift you as wheat, but I have prayed for you **that your faith would not fail."***

   My version of *"Be still and know that I am God"* is: "lie back in My arms and quiet your spirit. I'm doing My thing My way, and this nightmare will finally pass and you'll be more turned on to Me than ever before."

10. **Finally, understand that God's timing for your deliverance is a very important factor with God, and that His delays are not His denials.** For example, when Jesus delayed to come to Mary and Martha when their brother Lazarus was ill and finally died, Jesus had a greater plan,

which was to resurrect him (see John 11). Are we willing to wait for the timing that will bring the greatest glory to His name? Even if that means our circumstances may get worse, as well as be prolonged? Can we trust God's character to that degree?

I sought God on another occasion to tell me if the reason my healing is delayed is because that's the way more glory can come to His name. He answered by saying, "Turn to page 961 in your Bible." It was Acts 4 and I was arrested by verses 21 and 22: *"They all glorified God, for what had been done, for the man was over 40 years old on whom the miracle of healing had been performed."* At a later time, when in severe pain, I asked the same question. God answered by opening the Bible to me at exactly the same place.

Also, Y.W.A.M. leaders in England who were interceding for my healing at that time were directed by the Holy Spirit to the same Scriptures (see Acts 4:21-22). They wrote and shared them with me, with no knowledge that I had already been given them twice by the Lord.

About five years ago after seven years of suffering, the Holy Spirit quickened to me a Scripture in relation to the length of time I had waited since God first spoke to me that I would be completely healed. It was Daniel 10:1: *"The message was true, but the appointed time was long; and he understood the message."*

The clear understanding given to me was that God was confirming **again** that although I hadn't yet seen the fulfillment of the promised healing, I was to be encouraged that God had indeed spoken that I would be. Also, that there would be a long time between the initial promise, and it's fulfillment.

This communication from lover God brought great comfort to my heart and further confirmation to me that no matter what others said, or thought, and regardless of how many more years I would have to wait, God had an appointed time—His time—to set me free from my debilitating affliction and weakness.

I share this to particularly encourage others who are in long-term trials. You believe God spoke to you that deliverance would come, but as yet there is no fulfillment. And you're at a loss to understand why. My paraphrase of Daniel 10:1 is, "Hang in there, baby. I did speak to you, and one day you'll see the proof of My faithfulness. Remember, I didn't say *when* I'd show up, but just keep on trusting Me that I surely will."

We can be encouraged by the next two Scriptures that we don't stay in the fire, but we go through it: Zechariah 13:9 says, *"I will bring the one third through the fire. I will refine them as silver is refined and test them as gold is tested"*; and Isaiah 43:2 says, *"When you walk through the fire you will not be burned, nor shall the flame scorch you."* The daily devotional book, *Streams in the Desert*, has a poem that powerfully incorporates these promises:

> *When thou passest through the waters*
> *Deep the waves may be and cold*
> *But Jehovah is our refuge*
> *And His promise is our hold;*
> *For the Lord Himself hath said it,*
> *He, the faithful God and true;*
> *"When thou comest to the waters*
> *Thou shalt not go down, BUT, THROUGH."*

> *Seas of sorrow, seas of trial,*
> *Bitterest anguish, fiercest pain,*
> *'Rolling surges of temptation*
> *Sweeping over heart and brain'—*
> *They shall never overflow us*
> *For we know His word is true;*
> *All His waves and His billows*

He will lead us safely THROUGH.

Threatening breakers of destruction,
Doubt's insidious undertow,
Shall not sink us, shall not drag us
Out to ocean depths of woe:
For His promise shall sustain us,
Praise the Lord, whose Word is true!
We shall not go down or under,
For He saith, "Thou passest THROUGH."[45]

When we keep desiring that the Lord Jesus be glorified to the maximum, and our goal is to be more conformed into His image, we will keep worshiping Him, obeying Him, believing and trusting Him, whether in or out of the fire. We can be thankful for learning so much about our amazing God who is a consuming fire of holiness and love.

And we'll yet prove the truth of Psalm 66:10-12: *"For You O God have tested us; You have refined us as silver is refined. You brought us into the net; You laid affliction on our backs. You have caused men to ride over our heads; we went through fire and through water; but You brought us out to rich fulfillment.'* We'll have come to discover that the power of the Lord Jesus' person, presence, and purposes during the fire are stronger than the heat of the flames.

This should produce more of a burning and passionate love for Him, which, in turn, motivates us to qualify for the promise in Revelation 2:26: *"And he who overcomes and keeps My works until the end, to him I will give power over the nations."* Our choice to live this message determines not only our destiny here on earth but what God can trust us with in the ages to come.

For what are we living? This little bit of transient time on planet Earth, or, for the endless ages of eternity? We choose.

ENDNOTES

1. Paul Eshleman.

2. TransWorld Radio and F.E.B.C.

3. David Piper.

4. Marie Rigotti's letter to Joy Dawson.

5. Shirley Crow, "Change Me".

6. Andrew Woolsey, *The Biography of Duncan Campbell* (Hodder & Stoughton, 1974), 121-122.

7. Woolsey, *Duncan Campbell*, 129.

8. I remember reading these facts about the Hebrides revivals, which deeply impacted me, and I wrote them down. Unfortunately I didn't record the source of the information. All I know is that the source was very authentic.

9. Oswald J. Smith, *The Revival We Need* (Marshall, Morgan & Scott, Ltd.), 2-3.

10. David Brainerd, http://www.wholesomewords.org/missions/biobrainaerd4.html

11. Arthur Wallis, *The Rain From Heaven* (Hodder & Stoughton and Christian Literature Crusader), 17.

12. Frank Bartleman, *What Happened at Azusa Street* (Voice Christian Publications, Inc., 1962), 33.

13. Woolsey, *Duncan Campbell*, 134-135.

14. The two preceding paragraphs are adaptations from Edwin Orr's book, *The Eager Feet—Evangelical Awakenings 1790–1830* (Chicago: Moody Press), 31.

15. The three preceding paragraphs are adaptations from J. Edwin Orr's book, *The Fervent Prayer. The Impact of the Great Awakening of 1858* (Chicago: Moody Press), 48.

16. Oswald J. Smith, *The Revival We Need*, 3.

17. J. Edwin Orr, *Evangelical Awakenings 1900, Worldwide*, 193.

18. Orr, *Evangelical Awakenings*.

19. Edwin Orr, *The Re-Study of Revival and Revivalism*, 11.

20. Orr, *Revival and Revivalism*, 14-15.

21. Orr, *Eager Feet*, 60-61.

22. Lewis Drummond, *The Awakening That Must Happen*, 15-16.

23. Orr, *Revival and Revivalism*, 16.

24. Raymond Edman, *Finney Lives On* (Bethany Fellowship Inc.), 130.

25. Marie Monson, *The Awakening*, 28.

26. Monson, *The Awakening*, 28.

27. Monson, *The Awakening*, 33.

28. Monson, *The Awakening*, 87-88.

29. Monson, *The Awakening*, 109.

30. Monson, *The Awakening*, 85.

31. Monson, *The Awakening*, 110-111.

32. Edwin Orr, *Evangelical Awakenings During 1900*.

33. Raymond Edman, *Finney Lives On*, 69.

34. *This Is That* (Christian Literature Crusade), 11.

35. Mendell Taylor, *Exploring Evangelism*, 142.

36. Contact the international ministry of Open Doors to find out more about this book.

37. Testimony from a Spiritual Leader in Cuba.

38. This is an exact quote from Tozer, but unfortunately I have forgotten which of his many books I borrowed it from.

39. This is an exact quote from one of A.B. Simpson's books that I wrote down many years ago. I regret to say that I do not know the precise source.

40. I wrote this abridged version of Santosh's story based on material from Margaret Cleator's *The God Who Answers By Fire* (Gospel Communication, 1968).

41. *Strategic Times Journal*, Issachar Frontier Mission Strategies, October-December issue.

42. George Stormont, *Smith Wigglesworth: A Man Who Walked With God.*

43. Charles Spurgeon.

44. Frank Haughton, *Amy Carmichael of Dohnavur.*

45. This poem can be found in the devotional, *Streams in the Desert.* I obtained a copy of this poem from a friend, not from the original source, and therefore I have no other documentation for it.

Other Titles By Joy Dawson

Jesus the Model - the plumb line for Christian living

Becoming more like Jesus—radically real—we discover our greatest challenge and ultimate fulfillment.

Forever Ruined for the Ordinary

This exciting bok explains how to experience the adventure of hearing and obeying God's voice as a way of life.

Intercession, Thrilling and Fulfilling

An inspiring manual taking the reader to greater depths and breadth in effective prayer for others.

Intimate Friendship with God (revised edition)

This insightful best seller explains how God's standard of holiness affects every area of our lives.

Some of the Ways of God in Healing

If you have more questions than answers about healing, then this book is for you. Joy is ruthless in her pursuit of truth from God's Word.

Influencing Children to Become World Changers

Filled with wisdom, inspiration, and fascinating real-life stories, this practical book is a must-read for everyone who desires to impact children to enable them to reach their God-ordained destinies and help shape the world.

Obtainable from Christian bookstores or from: **Youth with a Mission**
11141 Osborne St., Lake View Terrace, CA 91342
818-896-2755 (phone), 818-897-6738 (fax)
Website: www.ywamla.org, E-mail: info@ywamla.org

Additional copies of this book and other
book titles from DESTINY IMAGE are
available at your local bookstore.

Call toll-free: 1-800-722-6774.

Send a request for a catalog to:

Destiny Image® Publishers, Inc.
P.O. Box 310
Shippensburg, PA 17257-0310

*"Speaking to the Purposes of God for This
Generation and for the Generations to Come."*

**For a complete list of our titles,
visit us at www.destinyimage.com**